Selection of Budapest Hotels and Restaurants

Where do you start? Choosing an hotel or restaurant in a place you're not familiar with can be daunting. To help you find your way amid the bewildering variety, we have made a selection of the best options in Budapest and the Lake Balaton area.

Our own Berlitz criteria have been price and location. In the hotel section, for a double room with bath without breakfast, "Higher-priced" means above Fts. 8,000; "Medium-priced" Fts. 4,000 to Fts. 7,500; "Lower-priced" about Fts. 3,000 to Fts. 4,000. Special features where applicable, plus regular business hours are also given.

As a rule, no extra service charges are added to the bills, but a tip of about 10 per cent is customary.

HOTELS

HIGHER-PRICED

(above Fts. 8,000)

Aquincum
Budapest IV
Arpád fejedelem útja 94
Tel: 188-6360; fax: 168-8872
At the site of the ancient Roman city, on the Danube.

Atrium Hyatt
Budapest V
Roosevelt tér 2
Tel: 138-3000; fax: 118-8659
Indoor gardens. Three restaurants. Conference centre.

Duna Intercontinental
Budapest V
Apáczai Csere János u. 4
Tel: 118-2203; fax: 118-4973
On the Danube. Superb views of Buda Castle.

Hilton
Budapest I
Hess András tér 1/3
Tel: 175-1000; fax: 175-1000
Beautiful setting and views.

Thermal
Budapest XIII, Margitsziget
Tel: 132-1100; fax: 153-3029
Spa hotel on Danube island.

MEDIUM-PRICED

(Fts. 4,000–Fts. 7,500)

Béke
Budapest VI
Teréz krt. 43
Tel: 132-3300; fax: 153-3380
Downtown. First class amenities.

Buda Penta
Budapest I
Krisztina korút 41/43
Tel: 156-6333; fax: 155-6964
Near castle and park.

Flamenco
Budapest XI
Tas Vezér u. 7
Tel: 161-2250; fax: 165-8007
Spanish food, music and style.

Fórum
Budapest V
Apáczai Csere János u. 12/14
Tel: 117-8088; fax: 117-9808
Modern. Roof swimming pool.

Gellért
Budapest XI
Szt. Gellért tér 1
Tel: 185-2200; fax: 166-6631
Excellent spa facilities.

Grand Hotel Hungária
Budapest VII
Rákóczi út 90
Tel: 122-9050; fax: 122-8029
Ideal transit hotel.

Nemzeti
Budapest VIII
József korút 4
Tel: 133-9160
Downtown. Nineteenth-century
dining traditions.

Novotel
Budapest XII
Alkotás u. 63-67
Tel: 186-9588; fax: 166-5636
Superb cuisine.

Olympia
Budapest XII, Eotvos út 40
Tel: 156-8011; fax: 156-8720
Swimming and tennis in forest
setting.

Ramada Grand Hotel
Budapest XIII, Margitsziget
Tel: 111-1000; fax: 153-3029
Mediaeval setting on Margaret
Island.

Royal
Budapest VII
Erzsébet korút 47/49
Tel: 153-3133; fax: 114-2122
Traditional hotel in heart of
town.

LOWER-PRICED

(Fts. 3,000–Fts. 4,000)

Aero
Budapest IX
Ferde u. 1/3
Tel: 127-4690; fax: 127-5825
Near airport.

Astoria
Budapest V
Kossuth Lajos u. 19
Tel: 117-3411; fax: 118-6798
Traditional hotel. Downtown.

Budapest
Budapest II
Szilágyi Erzsébet fasor 47
Tel: 115-3230; fax: 115-0496
Superb views on all sides.

Emke
Budapest VII
Akácfa u. 1/3
Tel: 122-9230
In lively city centre.

Erzsébet
Budapest V
Károlyi Mihály u. 11
Tel: 138-2111; fax: 118-9237
Hungarian cuisine.

Európa
Budapest II
Hárshegyi út 5/7
Tel: 176-7122
Excellent recreational facilities.

Expo
Budapest X
Dobi István u. 10
Tel: 184-2130
On Budapest International
Fairground.

Ifjúság
Budapest II
Zivatar u. 1/3
Tel: 135-3331
Economically priced.

Metropol
Budapest VII
Rákóczi út 58
Tel: 142-1173
Lively setting.

Palace
Budapest VIII
Rákóczi út 43
Tel: 114-2619
Hungarian food and gypsy music.

Rege
Budapest II
Pálos út. 2
Tel: 176-7950; fax: 176-7680
Recreation centre.
Entertainment.

Stadion
Budapest XIV
Ifjúság u. 1/3
Tel: 251-2222; fax: 251-2062
Near People's Stadium.

Taverna
Budapest V
Váci utca 20
Tel: 138-4999; fax: 118-7188
In the centre of the business district.

Volga
Budapest XIII
Dózsa Gyorgy út 65
Tel: 129-0200; fax: 140-8316
New catering centre.

LAKE BALATON AREA
(Lower- and medium-priced)

Annabella
Balatonfüred
Beloiannisz u. 25
Tel: 86/42-222
Cozy recreational complex.

Auróra
Balatonalmádi
Bajcsy-Zsilinszky út 14
Tel: 80/38-810
Near the lake. Country food.

Balaton
Siófok
Petofi-sétány 9
Tel: 84/10-695
Excellent food and wines.

Európa
Siófok, Petofi-sétány 15
Tel: 84/13-411
Near lake. Regional cuisine.

Hungária
Siófok, Petofi-sétány 13
Tel: 84/10-678
On lake shore. Beautiful views.

Lidó
Siófok
Petofi-sétány 11
Tel: 84/10-633
Hungarian cuisine and clientele.

Margaréta
Balatonfüred
Széchenyi u. 29
Tel: 86/43-824
Local food and wine.

Marina
Balatonfüred
Széchenyi u. 26
Tel: 86/43-644
Private beach. Wine tasting.

Neptun
Balatonfoldvár
Tel: 84/40-392
Peaceful setting. Excellent local wine.

RESTAURANTS

HIGH-PRICED

Alabdáros
Budapest I
Országház u. 2
Tel: 156-0851
Excellent choice of cuisine. Open from 7 p.m. to midnight.

Császárkert
Budapest III
Pacsirtamezo u. 30
Tel: 188-6137
Elegant surroundings. Open from 6 p.m. to 2 a.m.

Etoile
Budapest XIII
Pozsonyi u. 4

Tel: 112-2242
Elegant French restaurant. Open noon to midnight.

Gundel
Budapest XIV
Állatkerti út 2
Tel: 122-1002
Traditional cuisine. Open noon to 4 p.m. and 7 p.m. to midnight.

Légrády
Budapest V
Magyar u. 23
Tel: 118-6804
Gourmet food. Open from 7 p.m. to midnight.

Mátyás Pince
Budapest V
Március 15 tér 7
Tel: 118-1650
Hungarian cuisine, gypsy music. Open noon to 1 a.m.

Paradiso
Budapest XII
Istenhegyi u. 40/a
Tel: 156-1988
Elegant restaurant. Open from 7 p.m. to midnight.

Vadrózsa
Budapest II
Pentelei H. u. 15
Tel: 135-1118
Stylish, renowned restaurant. Open from 7 a.m. to midnight.

MEDIUM-PRICED

Apostolok
Budapest V, Kigyó u. 4/6
Tel: 118-3704
Good cuisine. Open from 10 a.m.
to midnight.

Aranyhordó
Budapest I, Tárnok u. 16
Tel: 156-6765
International cuisine. Open from
noon to midnight.

Aranyszarvas
Budapest I, Szarvas tér 1
Tel: 175-6451
Good wine list. Open from
6 p.m. to 2 a.m.

Borkatakomba
Budapest XXII
Nagyténéyi üt 67
Tel: 146-4859
Wide-ranging choice of
Hungarian wines. Open 5 p.m. to
midnight.

Fortuna
Budapest I, Hess András t. 4
Tel: 175-6857
International and Hungarian
cuisine. Open from 7 p.m. to
1 a.m.

Gambrinus
Budapest VII, Teréz krt. 104
Tel: 112-7631
Excellent choice of beer. Open
from noon to 3 p.m. and from
6 p.m. to midnight.

Kárpátia
Budapest V
Károlyi Mihály u. 4/8
Tel: 117-3596
Lively atmosphere. Open 11 a.m.
to 3 p.m., 6 to 11 p.m.

Kis Buda
Budapest II
Frankel Leo u. 34
Tel: 115-2244
Outstanding menu. Open from
noon to midnight.

Margitkert
Budapest II
Margit u. 15
Tel: 135-4791
Local cuisine, well prepared.
Open noon to midnight.

Ménes Csárda
Budapest V
Apáczai Csere J. u. 15
Tel: 117-0803
Traditional Hungarian dishes.
Open from noon to 1 a.m.

Pesta-Buda
Budapest I
Fortuna u. 1-3
Tel: 156-9849
Open from noon to 3 p.m. and
from 7 p.m. to midnight.

Posta Kocsi
Budapest III
Fo tér 2
Tel: 168-8701
Typically Hungarian cuisine.
Open from 7 p.m. to midnight.

Százéves
Budapest V
Pesti Barnabás u. 2
Tel: 118-3608
Traditional cuisine. Open
11.30 a.m. to midnight.

Vasmacska
Budapest III
Laktanya 3-5
Tel: 188-7123
Notably good cuisine.

Vén Buda
Budapest II
Erod u. 22
Tel: 115-3396
Excellent wine and cuisine. Open
from 5 p.m. to midnight.

Vigadó
Budapest V
Vigadó tér 2
Tel: 117-6222
Open from noon to midnight.

LOWER-PRICED

Aranymókus
Budapest XII
Istenhegyi u. 54
Tel: 155-9594
Open from noon to midnight.

Fenyogyongye
Budapest III
Szépvolgyi ut. 133
Tel: 168-8144
Tavern and inn situated in forest
park. Open noon to midnight.

Kaltenberg
Budapest IX
Kinizci u. 30-35
Tel: 118-9792
Freshly brewed beer. Open from
noon to midnight.

Kis Pipa
Budapest VII
Akácfa u. 38
Tel: 118-9792
Pleasant atmosphere. Open from
noon to midnight.

Kulacs
Budapest VII
Osváth u. 11
Tel: 112-3611
Interesting, varied menu. Open
from noon to 2 a.m.

Régi Országház
Budapest I
Országház u. 17
Tel: 175-1767
Intimate atmosphere, good
music. Open 11 a.m. to midnight.

Tabáki Kakas
Budapest I, Attila u. 27
Tel: 175-7165
Pleasant setting. Open from noon
to midnight.

Vadászkert
Budapest XIV
Erszébet Kiralyné u. 5
Tel: 163-6399
Notably good cuisine, venison
being the speciality. Open from
noon to midnight.

BERLITZ®

BUDAPEST

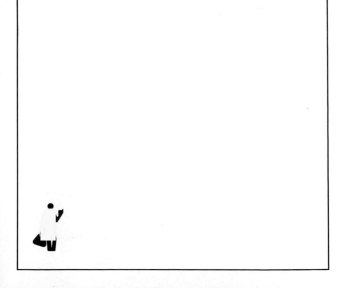

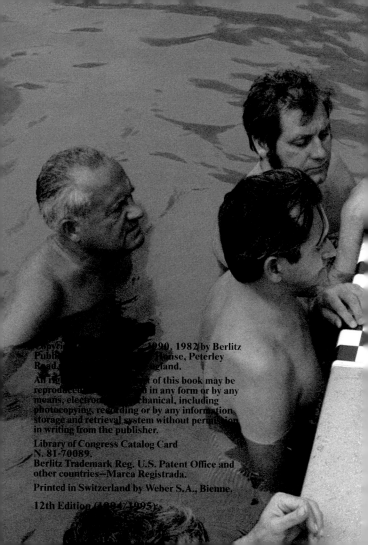

How to use our guide

- All the practical information, hints and tips that you will need before and during the trip start on page 102.

- For general background, see the sections Budapest and the Hungarians, p. 6, and A Brief History, p. 15.

- All the sights to see are listed between pages 24 and 74, with suggestions on daytrips from Budapest from page 74 to 85. Our own choice of sights most highly recommended is pinpointed by the Berlitz traveller symbol.

- Entertainment, nightlife and all other leisure activities are described between pages 85 and 94, while information on restaurants and cuisine is to be found on pages 95 to 101.

- Finally, there is an index at the back of the book, pp. 126–128.

Found an error or an omission in this Berlitz Guide? Or a change or new feature we should know about? Our editor would be happy to hear from you, and a postcard would do.

Although we make every effort to ensure the accuracy of all the information in this book, changes occur incessantly. We cannot therefore take responsibility for facts, prices, addresses and circumstances in general that are constantly subject to alteration.

Text: Ken Bernstein
Photography: Eric Jaquier; pp. 38, 61 (bottom) Claude Huber
Layout: Doris Haldemann
We wish to express our thanks to Prof. Joseph J. Hollos for his decisive role in guiding this project to fruition.
© Cartography: Cartographia, Budapest

Contents

Budapest and the Hungarians		6
A Brief History		15
What to See		24
	The Castle District	26
	Vantage Points	36
	Riverside Buda	39
	Margaret Island	48
	Pest	51
Excursions		
	Danube Bend	74
	Lake Balaton	80
What to Do		
	Shopping	85
	Sports	88
	For Children	91
	Nightlife	92
Wining and Dining		95
Blueprint for a Perfect Trip (Practical Information)		102
Index		126

Maps

	Castle District	25
	Budapest and the Hills	41
	Margaret Island	50
	Central Budapest	52
	Danube Bend	75
	Lake Balaton	81

Cover picture: Houses of Parliament
Photo, pp. 2–3: Széchenyi Baths

Budapest and the Hungarians

The Danube cuts through the heart of the city, distancing the historic Buda Hills from the elegant boulevards of Pest, yet linking and enhancing the beauty of the whole. And in part it's the dramatic setting that helps make Budapest one of Europe's most romantic cities. For romantic it undoubtedly is—you'll feel it, sense it, see it all around you. Love is in the Budapest air. Maybe it's those gypsy violins.

With a population above two million—ten times the size

of the country's next biggest town—Budapest is Hungary's economic and cultural capital as well as the political power-house. And it enjoys the lion's share of the tourist attractions and general excitement. In spite of its size and such metropolitan complications as the rush-hour traffic jams, the people of Budapest maintain a relaxed good cheer. They find time to smile, help a stranger, watch the city lights sparkling on the Danube.

Danube panorama with St. Gellért statue. Agriculture Hungarian-style keeps markets well-stocked.

The mighty river is crucial to Budapest's fascination; it also explains the city's very existence. Since prehistoric times, the Danube has provided settlers with plentiful fish and a means of communication. The Romans made it official nearly 2,000 years ago, when they chose the readily defensible hills of Budapest as the site for an important military garrison and provincial capital. They drew the line along the Danube, establishing the river as the last frontier between civilization and the barbarians. Inevitably, the barbarians won. But Budapest rose again... and again and again.

Since the Dark Ages, due to the tragic recurrence of invasion, war and revolution, the city has had to be rebuilt with disheartening frequency. The excavated vestiges of imperial Rome maintain a low profile on today's skyline. There are a few monuments to be approached with awe, but many restored buildings of advanced age, as well as admirable experiments of the 19th and 20th centuries. The most compelling slice of cityscape, in the Castle District of Buda, boasts a massive palace begun in the Middle Ages, the soaring barbed tower of an often-rebuilt 13th-century church, a joyous Gothic folly less than a century old, and a glassy Hilton hotel filling the gaps in an ancient monastery.

Although Trabants, Skodas and Ladas are still visible in the streets, more and more secondhand cars bought in Western Europe are influencing the general impression; and brandnew imported cars are in evidence too. Even Porsche has an agency in Budapest. McDonald's, Burger King, Wimpy, Pizza Hut, Kentucky Fried Chicken, Dairy Queen and other enterprises have branches in Hungary, and there are lots of shops selling proprietary articles such as Nike, Reebok, Adidas, Betty Barclay, Fruit of the Loom, Levis, and so on—so you'll find that there's no need to queue for luxury goods any more.

But for visitors interested in politics and economics, Hungary offers a look at the transition from socialism to capitalism. State-run factories and enterprises are giving way to private ownership. Foreign investment is on the increase, there is a stock market, and

8

Shoppers throng bustling Kígyó utca, a pedestrian street in Pest.

bankruptcy laws. A multi-party political system has evolved. Civil rights matter. Historians and journalists have come out from under the censor's yoke. And, in a country where the role of religion in society has caused pain and controversy, you'll find the churches packed every Sunday.

Budapest became the sum of its parts in 1873 with the amalgamation of the cities of Pest, Buda and Óbuda (Old Buda). The modern metropolis is divided into 22 administrative districts. As in Paris with its arrondissements, the number of the district tells you what kind of neighbourhood to expect. The first zone is historic, the second is rich in hillside villas, the third has Roman ruins and row after row of housing projects....

Because of architectural achievements old and new, and the profusion of trees, parks and gardens—and above all because of the Danube—the citizens love to look at Budapest from its many vantage points. Is the view of Buda from Pest more magnificent than the view of Pest from the heights of Buda? Is the grace of Elizabeth Bridge more fetching by day or by night? The people of Budapest are crazy about their bridges, perhaps because of their relative novelty. The first permanent span didn't go into service until 1849; the Chain Bridge was a great engineering achievement, for it crosses the Danube at a point where the river is wide and swift and prone to break up into ice-floes in the spring. Also, the older generation remembers Budapest at the end of World War II, when German demolition squads had blown up all the bridges and people had to rely on ferries and pontoons. So the sight of a hydrofoil skimming beneath the arching bridges rates a special sigh of appreciation.

Many an admiring glance is dedicated to the chic women of Budapest. Not all of them can look as glamorous as those ageless Hungarian exports, the Gabor sisters, but that same vivacity and flair often shines through. The government, aware of the importance of this natural resource, makes sure the city is well supplied with modern hairdressing establishments. They open as early as 6 a.m. for the convenience of customers who need a pick-me-up on the way to work.

The Hungarians conform to no stereotype in their

physical appearance. There are high-cheekboned blondes and round-faced brunettes, swarthy men with droopy moustaches and blue-eyed red-heads to confuse the issue. But, with middle age, most show the toll of all those strudel snacks and feasts, thickening around the middle in spite of the calisthenics classes so prominent on TV.

Visitors soon understand that in Budapest—as in Paris or Peking—good food plays an exceptionally important role in life. With all the gourmet restaurants and pastry shops, this is a perfect place to abandon a diet. But to sharpen the appetite, a stroll through the city is in order. You have to stay alert for architectural curiosities and surprises: colourful mosaics or sculpted ornaments on otherwise prosaic buildings; fountains and statues, historic and modern; an outdoor café just when you need it.

The more formal sights of Budapest are scattered all over the city's 200 square miles, so you can't expect to accomplish a lot on foot. Fortunately, public transport is highly developed and cheap. Peppy yellow tram-cars supplement the bright blue fleet of buses; and below ground, the metro system manages to be both hy-

gienic and efficient. The taxi service is good, with reasonable fares, but here as elsewhere it's the same old story: when it rains, there never seems to be a cab for hire.

However you get around, you'll find revered relics that tell the story of the city's development. There are the remains of the Roman town of Aquincum and authentic Turkish baths, still in operation. (The Ottoman Turks controlled Budapest for a century and a half.) A few Gothic churches have been restored, along with fine Baroque mansions. Under the Habsburgs, avenues of Baroque, neo-Classical and Eclectic buildings were laid out, and delightful experiments in Art Nouveau followed.

Budapest's many museums cover history, art and science, as well as such offbeat subjects as pharmacology and philately. Incidentally, the Budapest Fine Arts Museum may have the best collection of El Grecos and Goyas this side of Madrid. Theatres and concert halls maintain a busy programme of the performing arts. Though the language barrier blunts the appeal of the plays, you can take advantage of the abundance of good music. What other city of this size supports **11**

Figures from the past line up to form an imposing backdrop to the Heroes' Square.

two opera companies and four professional symphony orchestras? Not to mention chamber music, operetta and folk groups. In the land of Liszt and Bartók, music holds a special place of honour.

For a notoriously intellectual country, Hungary has a surprisingly big reputation in sports. This is based on many Olympic feats as well as memories, alas ever more distant, of a golden age of soccer. For the visitor there's plenty to watch, with international competi-tions in sports ranging from archery to wrestling. The big matches take place in the 73,000-seat Népstadion (People's Stadium), a sight in itself. In the same part of town are the racecourses—one for trotters, the other for flat racing. Hungary's famous horses also star in shows put on for tourists in the *puszta* or prairie. And horse-riding package holidays can be arranged.

Since prehistoric times a mystique has surrounded the hot springs of Budapest, of which there are well over 100. Locals and visitors plunge in for relief of various medical problems, or merely to unwind after a gruelling day. Aside from the steam, the baths have plenty of atmosphere, especially the Turkish ones, architectural monuments from the 16th and 17th centuries.

Some of this thermal energy has been utilized to provide the central heating for whole areas of Budapest. Warm radiators and double-glazed windows are essential defences against winter here. Officially, the January average is just below the freezing point, which is cold enough to ice the Danube and bring down the ear-flaps on fur hats. In July the mean temperature is a perfect 20°C (68°F). But it's never monotonous. The weather in summer is temperate but temperamental—subject to heat waves and sudden thunderstorms. Vacationers at Lake Balaton, Hungary's substitute for a sea, watch out for colourful rockets which the authorities launch to warn of approaching tempests.

Balaton, called the biggest lake in central Europe, attracts throngs of holiday-makers for swimming, boating and fishing. The south shore, with its endlessly shallow slope toward waist-deep water, is popular with parents of small children. The nearby villages and vineyards add to the picturesque appeal of Balaton, which makes for a busy day-trip from Budapest—or a relaxed week or two. Other organized excursions from Budapest go to the Danube Bend, the beautiful and historic area where the river changes its direction from eastbound to southerly. Closer to town, coach tours cover the Buda Hills; or you can do it yourself by public bus, cog railway and ski-lift.

Another popular excursion is called "Budapest by Night". You may be surprised to learn that nightlife tours are a standard feature of the tourist circuit. Budapest, "the Paris of the East", really does have a number of nightclubs, statuesque showgirls and all, plus various nightspots with live music and dancing. The guided tours promise to return celebrants to their hotels around 1 a.m., but the revelry continues around town until 5 in the morning. There are also a couple of gambling casinos, open until about 2 a.m., where roulette, baccarat, blackjack and one-armed bandits are now played in different foreign currencies.

For more sedate evenings out, there are Budapest's ma- **13** ny fine restaurants. Hungarian cuisine is first class, and much more varied than its reputation for paprika might indicate. Headed by the world-renowned Tokay, the roster of Hungarian wines is ample and attractive. And the after-dinner fruit brandies must be tried—and taken seriously.

Almost all of Budapest's restaurants come equipped with gypsy violin ensembles, strolling or stationary. The gushing music, under the influence of the wine and candlelight, may sound like an overdose of romance. But most visitors survive it, and many vow to return to Budapest to recapture the spell of the city that loves life.

Hungary: Facts and Figures

Geography: Area 35,909 square miles, slightly larger than Austria, but half the size of Oklahoma or Missouri. Landlocked Hungary borders on Austria, Slovakia, Romania, Slovenia and Croatia. Most of the terrain, a fertile plain, lies less than 655 feet above sea level. Hungary's biggest river, the Danube *(Duna),* forms the border with Slovakia in the north-west and then flows north to south through the country. Lake Balaton (area nearly 600 square kilometres) is central Europe's biggest lake.

Population: 10,337,000 (in 1992), of which one-fifth lives in Budapest. Aside from the Hungarians, there are small minorities of Germans, Slovaks, Southern Slavs and Romanians.

Government: Republic, multi-party system.

Economy: Transitional to free economy from centrally managed socialist system. Principal exports: agricultural and food products, bauxite, buses, consumer goods, machinery, pharmaceuticals.

Religion: Roman Catholic 65%, Protestant 25%, Jewish 0.3%, Greek Orthodox 0.3%.

Language: Hungarian. A widely understood second language is German, while the favourite of the younger generation is English.

A Brief History

By European standards the Hungarians are newcomers. They've lived in the Carpathian basin for less than 1,100 years—though they've invested that relatively brief tenure with a full quota of suffering, struggle and achievement.

As for the history of the land, the preamble goes back hundreds of thousands of years. Less than 40 miles west of Budapest, at the village of Vértesszőlős, human traces thought to be half a million years old have been excavated. The bones of these early men are displayed at the Hungarian National Museum.

The tribes that migrated to the area in prehistoric times brought new skills and tools which improved a hunter's odds, made farming feasible and permitted the rise of primitive industries. And tenuous trade routes were established which linked Hungary with more sophisticated societies thousands of miles away. At the start of the Iron Age, when the Scythians rode onto the scene, local workshops were producing weapons, pottery and jewellery.

In the 3rd century B.C. Hungary was occupied by Celtic warriors, retreating from defeat in Greece. They established a tribal centre atop Budapest's Gellért Hill, commanding the Danube. The Celts were responsible for major artistic advances and industrial innovations.

But the full benefits of western civilization didn't reach Hungary until the 1st century A.D. with the conquering legions of the Roman empire. The strategy of the Emperor Augustus (27 B.C.–A.D. 14) pushed the north-east frontier of the empire to the Danube. By the 2nd century perhaps 20,000 Roman soldiers were deployed along the river between Vienna and Budapest alone, manning the main line of defence against the barbarians.

To command and coordinate this long, exposed perimeter, the Romans built Aquincum, a military camp which soon spawned civilian suburbs laid out as straight as troops on parade. In A.D. 106, the outpost became the capital of the Roman province of Lower Pannonia. The importance of Aquincum can be judged by the magnitude and beauty of the Roman vestiges unearthed in widely separated areas of present-day Budapest.

The remains of the centre of the civil city—shrines, public

baths, markets, workshops and villas—run alongside the suburban railway tracks. Every day, coachloads of school-children are led through the maze of surviving walls and restored columns. A mile away, the students of one Budapest school don't have to go anywhere to study ancient Rome. Valuable mosaics have been left exactly where they turned up during the construction of the building: in the basement and next door in what would otherwise have been the school playground.

When the over-stretched Roman empire faltered, tribes as fearsome as the Vandals and Huns moved in for the kill. The Dark Ages enveloped Aquincum early in the 5th century when the city fell to Hun warriors. But the driving force of the conquest, the mighty Attila, died in 453, and other tribes overthrew the Huns. In the age of great migrations, waves of nomads pushed, or were pushed, ever westward. For better or worse, the only period of relative stability came during occupation by the Avars. But they, too, were conquered.

A proud heritage: Óbuda's Roman theatre, Esztergom's religious art.

The Hungarians

The tribes which finally triumphed—the traditional date is 896—had wandered a long way from their home base between the River Volga and the Ural mountains. (Related tribes from the same homeland ended up in Finland. Specialists label both the Finnish and Hungarian peoples, and their strange, mutually incomprehensible languages, as Finno-Ugric.) The first great Hungarian leader, Prince Árpád, founded a dynasty which led Hungary into statehood. Árpád's tribe was known as the Magyars; later, all Hungarians were to call themselves Magyars, and the tribe's name became the name of the country and its language, as well.

On Christmas Day in the memorable year of A.D. 1000, Hungary crowned its first king, Stephen I. Like his father, Prince Géza, King Stephen accepted Christianity and the authority of the pope; he was to attain sainthood.

A landmark of 1222, the Golden Bull—a sort of Magyar Magna Carta—spelled out the rights of the citizens, nobles and freemen alike. But civilization suffered a tragic setback in 1241, when the country was overrun by Mongol hordes. It was the first of

many military and political disasters to afflict Hungary over the centuries, into modern times.

King Béla IV set about reviving the young nation from the wreckage. He granted a new charter for the reawakening city of Pest and, across the Danube, founded the town

Challenging Tongue

Hungarian is such a distinctive, intricate language that most foreigners despair of finding their way through the maze of conjugations, suffixes and diacritical marks. Furthering the feeling of foreignness, only a handful of international words carry over into Hungarian. You may recognize *garázs* (garage), *posta* (post office), *trolibusz* (trolleybus) and a few more, but even such universal words as hotel, police and restaurant are different in Hungarian.

On the other hand, several Magyar words have enhanced other languages: czardas (from the music played at the wayside inn called a *csárda*); goulash and paprika; and *coach*—a four-wheeled carriage developed in the 15th century in the Hungarian village of Kocs (pronounced coach)!

other Christian peoples as well. János Hunyadi, the viceroy of Hungary, led the armies which turned back a long-threatening and seemingly invincible Turkish juggernaut. His 1456 triumph at Nándorfehérvár (now Belgrade) is remembered to this day by Catholics all over the world; and in commemoration, church bells ring and the Hungarian radio even relays the toll of the angelus every noontime.

The son of János Hunyadi, known as Matthias Corvinus, reigned as Hungary's king from 1458 to 1490, a golden age of civic and intellectual development. Buda became an advanced centre of Renaissance culture and Pest flourished in trade and industry. King Matthias employed Italian artists to expand and beautify the Royal Palace on Castle Hill and he commissioned exquisite illuminated volumes to fill its library.

16th-Century Defeats

With the death of Matthias, feuding noblemen squabbled over the succession, reversing the movement towards national progress and security. An army of peasants, led by György Dózsa, rose in rebellion in 1514, but the insurrec-

of Buda on a plateau which he prudently enclosed within walls.

With the end of the Árpád dynasty in 1301, a series of foreign kings ruled Hungary— a cosmopolitan royal roster drawn from all over Europe. In the middle of the 15th century, a hero emerged to rally not only the Hungarians, but

Gül Baba's tomb: one of the well-preserved relics of Turkish rule.

tion failed and the leaders were tortured to death; harsh laws were enacted to reinstate the ancient deprivations of the serfs.

All the while, the Turks had been massing for war against a weakened Hungary. The fateful battle was fought near Mohács in southern Hunga-ry in 1526. Hungary's King Louis II died, as did much of the scanty army he led. In a slow-motion disaster, the Turks finally occupied Buda in 1541. The nation was demoralized and dismembered: the north and west fell to the Habsburg empire, Transylvania became a so-called independent principality under Turkish auspices, and central Hungary bowed under direct Turkish rule.

Occupation by the Otto- **19**

mans ushered in an era of inertia, rather than oppression. During the century and a half of Ottoman rule, little was accomplished apart from the construction of fortifications and public baths. Visitors were appalled to find Buda decaying, and an official who went to the other side of the river despaired: "Alas, poor Pest! Pestilence should be thy name". But the worst was yet to come. Pest and later Buda were subjected to long, devastating sieges before the Turks were finally routed by the armies of allied Christian powers. In 1686 Buda, "liberated", lay in ruins.

Under the Habsburgs

With the dominion of the pashas at an end, Hungary found itself under the stern administration of the Habsburgs. Dissatisfaction festered, and in 1703 Hungarians went to war for independence. The leader was a Transylvanian prince with a handlebar moustache, Ferenc Rákóczi II. Outnumbered and betrayed, the Hungarians lost the struggle in 1711.

The 18th century was a period of Germanisation, a golden age for the Hungarian aristocracy, who enjoyed all the advantages of the Habsburg court, but one of oppression for the backward peasant classes, who were burdened with extra taxation to pay for the reconstruction of the country. At the end of the century revolutionary ideas spread from France, and the early years of the 19th century became known as the reform period, culminating in a new war for independence from the Habsburgs. According to popular tradition the initial rebellion of 1848 was led by a romantic, radical poet, the 25-year-old Sándor Petőfi and a group of young intellectuals. To crush the insurrection, Emperor Franz Joseph I summoned help from the Czar of Russia. The combined Austrian and Russian armies finally triumphed in August 1849. The revolutionary statesman Lajos Kossuth, who had headed a provisional government, and other leaders of the independence struggle fled the country.

Defeat was followed by political repression, but economic advancement gradually resumed. Soon after peace returned to Hungary, the prodigious Chain Bridge inaugurated uninterrupted year-round traffic across the Danube; a railway was opened between Pest and Vienna; and trading began on the Pest stock exchange. In 1873 the cities of Pest, Buda and Óbuda—with a combined population approaching 300,000—merged into the metropolis of Budapest, big and strong enough to be the nation's undisputed capital.

A new political framework had been created in 1867. Under a compromise designed to curtail home-rule agitation, the Austro-Hungarian empire was established. Hungary was granted its own government, but key ministries were shared with the Austrians. The Dual Monarchy, as it was called, oversaw the development of modern Budapest with its proud boulevards and buildings. It also set the stage for the 20th century's jolting political changes.

Into War and Revolution
Hungary fought World War I on the losing side. As part of the Austro-Hungarian empire, the country was obliged to aid its German allies. Hundreds of thousands of Hungarian troops died on two fronts, and at home the hardships multiplied.

In October 1918, the monarchy was toppled by what is now referred to as the Bourgeois Democratic Revolution. King Charles IV of Austria-Hungary, crowned Hungarian king in Buda's Matthias Church less than two years earlier, was deposed to make way for the Hungarian Republic.

This was soon displaced by a short-lived Hungarian Soviet Republic. Among the leaders were Hungarians who had participated in the Bolshevik revolution and army veterans who had become communists while prisoners of war in Russia. The proclamation of a Hungarian dictatorship of the proletariat was vigorously opposed in many circles. It was overthrown after only 133 days in power.

The new right-wing regime, headed by Admiral Miklós Horthy, initiated a purge. Meanwhile, reprisals of another sort were laid out in the Treaty of Trianon (1920), which punished Hungary for its role in World War I. About two-thirds of Hungary's territory was handed over to its neighbours. Shrunken in size and spirit, torn by strife and crippled by economic problems, Hungary heard a vengeful voice from across the border: Adolf Hitler was promising a new order.

Hungary slipped into World War II in a series of small, reluctant steps: German troops were allowed to cross Hungarian territory and a Hungarian force was sent to help Hitler fight the Soviet Union. But the Horthy government nimbly avoided total involvement on the Axis side until March 1944 when the Germans occupied Hungary. This precluded a separate peace.

As the Soviets moved closer to Budapest, a Hungarian fascist regime led by Ferenc Szálasi was installed to support the Germans in a fight to the

In the early days of communism, rousing posters rallied workers.

Celebrated Magyars

Because of the obscurity of their language, perhaps, Hungarian authors and poets have won little fame abroad. Conversely, when it comes to universal abstractions, the country has produced more than its share of notables.

In science, several Hungarians won fame in the United States: Nobel laureate Albert Szent-Györgyi, atomic pioneers Leo Szilárd and Edward Teller, and cybernetician John von Neumann. Péter Goldmark cut his niche in history by inventing the LP record.

Hungarians have played second fiddle to nobody in the musical world since Franz Liszt opened his academy in his Budapest home. Twentieth-century composers, conductors and soloists from Hungary include Béla Bartók, Zoltán Kodály, Antal Doráti, Eugene Ormándy, Sir George Solti and Joseph Szigeti.

Hungarian artists, too, have achieved international recognition: László Moholy Nagy, famed for his constructions; Marcel Breuer, architect and designer associated with the Bauhaus; and Victor Vasarely, the Op art painter.

One field in which Hungarians have excelled from the beginning is the cinema. Among legendary film-makers, Sir Alexander Korda was born Sándor Korda, and director Michael Curtiz began his career as Mihály Kertész. Some memorable actors with Hungarian roots are Leslie Howard, George Sanders and Béla Lugosi.

---

death. The final siege went on for weeks. When the Red Army finally secured all of Budapest on February 13, 1945, the capital could count only one out of every four buildings intact.

In and Out of the Red

Post-war Hungary was transformed from a republic (1946) into a People's Republic (1949). The government and party were led by hardlining Mátyás Rákosi, who was finally dismissed in 1956. It was a year of tumultuous change.

On October 23 a students' and workers' demonstration was met by police bullets. The protest snowballed into a popular uprising. Within days an interim coalition headed by Imre Nagy proclaimed Hungary's neutrality and withdrawal from the Warsaw Pact. On November 4, Soviet tanks entered Budapest. The Soviets installed János Kádár as head of a new government. The uprising was suppressed. It caused a heavy toll of life and property; and some 200,000 Hungarians fled to the West. Nagy and other independence leaders were hanged.

Gradually ideological severities were relaxed and millions of Hungarians were allowed to take holidays in the West. Yet the "goulash communism" economy failed to meet its full potential.

As new winds of *perestroika* blew in from Moscow in the late 1980s, Kádár was pensioned off. Hungary began dismantling the barbed wire along the Austrian border. A whirlwind of reforms followed as a multi-party democracy took shape.

On the 31st anniversary of Imre Nagy's execution he and four colleagues were reburied with honours, as were, symbolically, 300 executed freedom fighters.

Official name changes told the historic events in few words: the communist party changed its name to Socialist, and the nation from People's Republic to Republic.

The fascinating new political and economic experiments are open to inspection, as are the monuments to past trials and glories.

What to See

Buda and Pest look like pieces from two different jigsaw puzzles which fit quite by chance. Hilly Buda is the last frontier of the Transdanubian mountains; in Pest, across the river, begins the Great Plain, stretching east as flat as Kansas.

The attractions are too varied and widely dispersed to absorb in a quick, easy survey. Though the various coach excursions serve as a useful introduction, the city is most easily approached by degrees—a bit of Buda and a part of Pest, then back across the river again.

For reasons of organization, though, we have split the city into halves along the course of the Danube. We begin in Buda, covering the Castle District, the hills beyond, ancient Óbuda and other riverside precincts on the right bank. Then over to Pest with its boulevards, shops and museums. In between, we cast a glance at Margaret Island, a quiet green isle equidistant from the urban pressures of Buda and Pest.

The best place to start, most would agree, is in the Buda Castle District, with its concentration of history and art... and a view that's not to be missed.

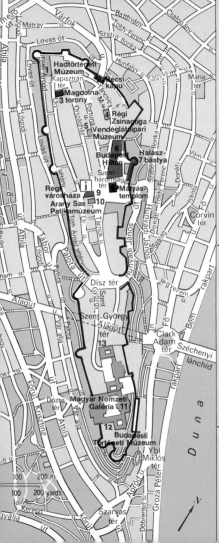

CASTLE DISTRICT

1. Military History Museum
2. Vienna Gate
3. Church of St. Mary Magdalene Tower
4. Former Synagogue
5. Catering Museum
6. Budapest Hilton Hotel
7. Fishermen's Bastion
8. Matthias Church
9. Former Town Hall
10. Golden Eagle Pharmaceutical Museum
11. Museum of Recent History
12. Hungarian National Gallery
13. Budapest Museum of History

Map-reading Key

körút	boulevard
köz	alley
rakpart	quay
tér	square
út	street
utca (u.)	street
útja	street

Note that many street names in Budapest, and throughout Hungary, are being changed. It is advisable to get the latest street map from the tourist office, see p.122.

   Museums

   Churches

Tourist Sights

   Tourist Information

The Castle District

This fascinating zone of cobbled streets, hidden gardens and medieval courtyards hovers above the rest of Budapest on a long, narrow plateau. Dozens of historic and beautiful buildings are concentrated here. Every second house, it seems, bears a plaque identifying it as a *műemlék* (monument). You can walk uphill from the river—or ride the vintage funicular *(sikló)* between a terminus at Clark Ádám tér and the Royal Palace.

The southern part of the plateau is occupied by the

palace, but we begin in the larger northern district, where 14th- and 15th-century aristocrats and artisans, civic and church officials resided.

The spire of **Mátyás-templom** (Matthias Church) towers gracefully over the old town. Here the 15th-century King Matthias wed Beatrice of Aragon. Founded by King Béla IV in the 13th century, the parish Church of Our Lady is also known as the coronation church. The Emperor Franz Joseph I was crowned here as king of Hungary in

In the Castle District (left), an orchestra plays in the open air.

1867, to the tune of Liszt's *Coronation Mass,* composed for the occasion. Nowadays a symphony orchestra and chorus perform classical religious works every Sunday at 10 a.m. mass.

During the Turkish occupation, the church was converted into the city's main mosque. Today visiting Hungarians pause reverently at the **Loreto Chapel,** in the south-west corner of the church, to regard a red marble statue of the Virgin. According to legend, the Turks buried the statue inside one of the chapel walls, but the figure made a miraculous reappearance during the siege of 1686. The pasha's troops took this as a signal that their time was up and prepared to surrender Buda.

The church was rebuilt in Baroque style after the return of the Christian forces; in the 19th century it was totally reconstructed along neo-Gothic lines. This is the version which was reassembled during the long restoration programme that made good the destruction of World War II. The unusual abstract designs which decorate the interior and roof of the church date from the 19th-century refurbishing; the motifs are Hungarian, not Turkish.

The **church museum,** on the premises, contains medieval stone carvings, sacred relics, historic vestments and works of religious art. Replicas of the Hungarian royal crown and coronation jewels are displayed, but you can view the genuine articles in Pest (see p. 65). The museum begins in the crypt and rambles up and around the church, offering at one spot an excellent view down onto the nave.

In the centre of Szentháromság tér (Trinity Square), on which the church stands, a votive column crowded with statues of saints and angels recalls a bubonic plague epidemic of the 18th century. The survivors built the monument in gratitude for being spared.

The other buildings facing the square are very much a mixed bag. On the north side, a neo-Gothic structure put up at the beginning of the 20th century now serves as a residence hall for students. On the west side, a modern whitewashed brick building, a latter-day reflection of the surrounding architecture, houses a centre for visiting foreign journalists. Outside stands a contemporary statue of a long-haired man, nude but for his hat, holding a horn with which to broadcast the latest news.

The Baroque two-storey white building with a jutting corner balcony is the former Town Hall. Below the balcony there's a statue of Pallas Athena, who carries a shield emblazoned with the coat of arms of the town of Buda.

A much grander monument rises on the far side of Matthias Church—an equestrian statue of King (and Saint) Stephen I, who made Hungary a Christian country. He wears both a crown and a halo.

Halászbástya (Fishermen's Bastion), on the eastern edge of Castle Hill, could pass as an authentic medieval monument in a remarkable state of repair. Actually, this Disneyesque array of turrets, terraces and arches was built at the beginning of the 20th century, just for fun. From here, the views over the Danube are glorious. The architect even provided arches at every turn, so photographers can hardly avoid artistic framing of their shots of the river, its bridges and the Pest skyline across the way.

Incidentally, you might well wonder why ramparts at this altitude should refer to fishermen. It seems that the area behind the church was the site of a medieval fish market; and in the 18th century, local fishermen were responsible for defending the fortifications.

Turning away from the Danube: the view westward from Fishermen's Bastion focuses on the startling and controversial six-storey reflective-glass façade of the **Budapest Hilton Hotel.** Hungarian architect Béla Pintér took the bold approach in his design for a modern hotel wedged between historic monuments. The hotel's main façade, facing Hess András tér, integrates the remains of a 17th-century Jesuit college formerly on the site. Parts of an adjoining 13th-century abbey have also been incorporated into the building. An ancient milestone uncovered during the excavation of the site is displayed in the lobby; it marked the boundary of the Roman empire.

Hess András tér is named after the man who ran Buda's first printing shop, right here, in the 1470s. (Like the Chinese, the Hungarians put the last name first; we would call the printer András Hess.) The statue in the little square honours Pope Innocent XI for his help in organizing the army which finally routed the Turks from Buda. Notice the amusing bas-relief of a hedgehog on the house at No. 3; in the 18th century, it was an inn called the Red Hedgehog.

Historic Streets

The quaint Castle District lends itself to relaxed roaming with no hard and fast itinerary. Only four streets wide at its most expansive, the plateau is easily covered on foot. Here are some of the highlights to look for, starting with the easternmost street and working towards the western ramparts.

Táncsics Mihály utca. No. 7: Beethoven lived for a while (in 1800) in this solid old building. Next door, at No. 9, an 18th-century ammunition dump became a 19th-century prison which held, among others, the statesman Lajos Kossuth and the politician, and journalist Mihály Táncsics. No. 16: note the 18th-century religious mural between the bow windows upstairs. No. 26: just inside the doorway ancient Jewish tombstones are displayed. This house served as a synagogue *(Régi Zsinagóga)* from the end of the 14th century and now contains an exhibition of architectural and artistic remains.

At the northern end of the

Reflected in the glass façade of the Budapest Hilton, the fanciful towers of Fishermen's Bastion look even more surreal.

street, **Bécsi kapu** (Vienna Gate) provides a reminder of the walled city of yore, although the actual gate is a reconstruction. A couple of appealing, intricately decorated 18th-century houses add to the charm of the square. Thomas Mann lived at No. 7 from 1935 to 1936.

Fortuna utca. The house at No. 4, a hotel in the 18th and 19th centuries, has been given over to the **Hungarian Museum of Commerce and Catering** *(Magyar Kereskedelmi és Vendéglátóipari Múzeum).* The furnishings of historic hotel rooms, restaurants and coffee houses are assembled here, along with original menus, table settings and waiters' uniforms.

Like the rest of the district, this street has had to be rebuilt after every war, siege and invasion. Following the expulsion of the Turks, the medieval ruins were used as building blocks for new Baroque houses. After the devastation of World War II, many minor but attractive details of the architecture were lovingly restored.

Tárnok utca. This southerly extension of Fortuna utca contains a number of fine Baroque buildings. At No. 14, now an "espresso" restaurant, **31**

the upper storey juts out, as it did in the Middle Ages. The geometric frescoes on the front walls date from the 16th century. Up the street, at No. 18, an 18th-century chemist's shop called the **Golden Eagle** *(Arany Sas)* now serves as a museum. The exhibits cover the development of pharmaceutical science from ancient times, both in Hungary and around the world. Some of the architectural elements of the shop itself, begun in the 15th century, are also of interest.

Országház utca, which means Houses of Parliament Street, is not, as you might think, on the wrong side of the river. Parliamentary sessions took place in the building at No. 28 at the turn of the 19th century. It now belongs to the Academy of Sciences. At No. 2 Országház utca, a restaurant occupies what was once a grand 15th-century mansion; the courtyard, reminiscent of a medieval cloister, is noteworthy. Several other buildings on this street incorporate picturesque medieval features, sometimes just beyond the doorway; don't be shy about peering into courtyards, just in case.

Úri utca. This street is a treasure-trove of medieval vestiges. In the entryways of Nos. 31, 32, 35, 36, 38 and 40, among other houses, you'll find groups of sediles—built-in seats. The 14th-century dwelling at No. 31 retains the original stone window frames. Whatever their ages, virtually all of the buildings in the area maintain the same roof-line, but differing colour schemes and embellishments make each one distinctive.

At the top end of Úri utca stands a rather bleak but venerable tower *(Magdolna-torony),* all that remains of the Church of St. Mary Magdalene. There has been a church on this spot since the 13th century. During the Turkish occupation, it was the only one left in Christian hands; the Catholics and Protestants shared the premises. The church suffered particularly grave damage in the last days of World War II, when the German army high command was holding out in the district. Miraculously, the Gothic tower escaped destruction.

Tóth Árpád sétány. This promenade along the western ramparts of the Castle District offers panoramas of the Buda Hills, rather than any outstanding monuments. And in the valley below you can see some metropolitan aspects of Buda, including the white im-

Many charming buildings in the Castle District date back to medieval times.

mensity of Southern Railway Station *(Déli pályaudvar)* and the cylindrical glass tower of the Budapest Hotel.

The northern end of the walk is cluttered with cannon—historic cast-iron guns laid out on display. The building at No. 40, much bigger than it looks, houses the

Museum of Military History *(Hadtörténeti Múzeum).* The exhibits range from pikes, swords and crossbows to a self-propelled missile launcher and a Mig-21 (parked in the courtyard). Selected documents and relics illustrate Hungary's efforts at self-defence over the centuries. **33**

The Royal Palace

Returned to its former splendour, the Royal Palace *(Budavári Palota)* monopolizes the southern skyline of the plateau. Construction began rather modestly under Béla IV in the 13th century, but succeeding monarchs were intent on impressing their countrymen.

Under the Ottoman empire the palace fell into disrepair and the remains were destroyed in the siege of 1686. During the 18th and 19th centuries reconstruction, renovation and expansion turned the building into approximately the neo-Baroque monument of today. But it had to be rebuilt from the ground up after the siege of 1945, when the palace served as command post for the German occupation forces. Earlier it had been the headquarters and residence of the reviled Admiral Horthy. But in spite of this chequered recent history, the palace has been restored with every care. And in fact it's probably better than ever, for out of the ruins came revelations of past glories.

To reach the palace, its fortifications and museums, you can either descend on foot from Dísz tér, in the southern part of the Castle District, or take a long walk up through the nicely landscaped grounds from Szarvas tér, near the complex road system on the west side of Elizabeth Bridge. If you walk along the Szarvas tér route, notice the "turbaned" Turkish gravestones on the hillside.

The solid stone walls of the restored fortifications guarding the southern approaches to the palace are now curtained with ivy. You can climb the spiral stairs to the ramparts for delightful Danube views. Within the palace complex are the national library and three museums.

The **Budapest Museum of History** *(Budapesti Történeti Múzeum)* occupies the Baroque south wing. This exhibition throws light on 2,000 years of the city's history. Displays include Roman statues, early Magyar saddles and weapons, Turkish utensils and 19th- and 20th-century Hungarian documents and photographs. During the most recent reconstruction programme, forgotten floors of the palace were discovered beneath the parts known before the war. The restored medieval passageways, fortifications and gardens now form part of the museum. Important sculptures

View from the top: Buda's Royal Palace surveys Pest, across the way.

from the 14th and 15th centuries also were uncovered, and they are on view in the Gothic Knights' Hall and the Royal Chapel. The sound of Gregorian chants coming from loudspeakers hidden in the chapel underlines the medieval aura.

The **Hungarian National Gallery** *(Magyar Nemzeti Galéria)* is installed in the central area of the palace, under the dome; the entrance faces the Danube. Within the bare historic walls, an impressive modern museum was created. Hungarian painters and sculptors from the Middle Ages onwards are represented. The artist best known abroad is the 19th-century painter Mihály Munkácsy, celebrated for his vast output of family scenes, portraits, landscapes and melancholy historical compositions. Note, too, the Impressionist Pál Szinyei Merse. He was the first Hungarian impressionist. Other artists to look for: Tivadar Csontváry-Kosztka, self-taught creator of huge landscapes, and Károly Ferenczy, another pioneer of impressionism.

In the north wing of the palace, the former Museum of the History of the Hungarian Working Class now is devoted to temporary exhibits, often on recent historical themes.

Vantage Points

Gellért-hegy (Gellért Hill) rises only 770 feet above sea level, but it looms right alongside the Danube, providing a perfect vantage point. The **panorama** of Pest and Buda, the bridges and river traffic suggest the short answer to the mystery of Budapest's universal appeal: the city is simply beautiful.

The hill and the district are named after the Italian missionary, St. Gerard (in Hungarian, Gellért), who converted many Hungarians to Christianity. His success was mostly posthumous, for his efforts were cut short when militant heathens threw him off the hillside into the Danube. A statue of the saint stands on the eastern slope at the approximate spot from which his martyrdom was launched.

At the summit of Gellért Hill sprawls a fortress with a deceptively ancient look about it. The **Citadella** (Citadel) was built in the middle of the last century. In the final struggle of World War II, the occupying German army held out here. In recent years, the renovation of the citadel has been earnestly pursued. The once-menacing walls, nearly 10 feet thick, now encircle a restaurant, café and hotel.

The conspicuous modern addition to the hilltop, a gargantuan Liberation Monument, honours the Soviet troops who ousted the German occupiers in 1945.

On the slopes below the Citadel lies a modern park, Jubileumi-park, a focus for patriotic occasions, as well as everyday recreation.

An extraordinary monument in the hillside is a cave converted into a chapel. It belongs to the much-persecuted Order of St. Paul, the only monastic body of Hungarian origin. It was reopened in 1989 after 38 years.

The Buda Hills

Now for some alternatives to city sightseeing for visitors who need a break from historic monuments. Excursions to the chain of wooded hills rising west of the Danube make a pleasant change from metropolitan hubbub.

A cog railway *(fogaskerekű vasút)* chugs to **Sváb-hegy** (Liberty Hill) from a terminal across the road from the Hotel Budapest. Comfortable modern trains built in Austria ascend through suburban greenery, past admirable villas and gardens, into open spaces —ski country in season.

Near the last stop of the cog railway, the **Children's Railway** *(Széchenyi-hegyi Gyermekvasút),* run by youngsters, begins its 7½-mile route. The narrow-gauge line traverses what would seem to be unexplored forest—but for the well-marked hiking trails all along the way. School-children in smart uniforms work as station-masters, switchmen, ticket-sellers and conductors; only the engine-drivers are adults.

Summer sightseers take over the ski-lift *(libegő)* for a "flight" of about a mile. The lower terminus is at 93 Zugligeti út, and the trip ends near the top of János-hegy (János Hill), altitude 1,735 feet. A look-out tower on the hilltop surveys a radius of more than 45 miles— but misty skies often blur that far horizon.

North of János-hegy and nearly as high (1,630 feet), Hármashatár-hegy provides another good look-out point for views of Budapest and the Danube. No funicular or other exotic means of transport goes to the top, but some interesting vehicles leave the hill in the opposite direction. The wind currents here make Hármashatár Hill an effective starting point for hang-gliders.

Sas-hegyi Természetvédelmi Terület (Eagle Hill Nature

Reserve), surrounded on all sides by the city, is described as a living outdoor museum. Nature lovers can try to identify the rare species of flowers, butterflies, birds... even snakes amid unusual rock formations. This hilltop sanctuary opens week-ends only; the rest of the time the flora and fauna have Sas-hegy all to themselves.

Admire the view from the Citadel. Or go for a ride on the Children's Railway. A school girl serves as conductor... but adults drive the trains.

Riverside Buda

After the aerial perspectives, the view from the river bank becomes more meaningful. People on the Pest quays never tire of gazing across the Danube to the skyline of Citadel and castle. Less obviously, from the Buda side the view of sophisticated though dead-level Pest has its share of curiosities and delights. And from either side, the bridges themselves, always in sight, add to the allure, stitching together the disparate halves of Budapest.

The area of prime interest to tourists extends north

from Szabadság híd (Liberty Bridge), opened in 1896 as the Franz Joseph Bridge. On the Buda side, the bridgehead is Szent Gellért tér (St. Gellért Square). The ponderous old **Gellért Hotel,** inaugurated in 1918, was badly damaged in the war but dutifully restored to its original Art Nouveau design. By no accident, the hotel was built alongside ancient hot springs and it remains a popular centre for medicinal and thermal baths. The outdoor swimming pool, with its artificial waves, is also an excellent facility.

The steep hillside comes right down to the river road as it runs north from the Gellért, finally retreating at the approaches to Elizabeth Bridge. Here is the Rudas fürdő (Rudas Baths) which has been in business for 400 years. Though the building has been destroyed, rebuilt, enlarged and much tampered with over the centuries, a graceful Turkish dome still rises over one octagonal pool, creating a wonder of geometric contrasts as sunlight filters through openings in the cupola. The radioactive water here is also said to make a therapeutic drink.

Of all Budapest's bridges, the lightest on its feet is Erzsé-

bet híd (Elizabeth Bridge), a 1960s successor to a turn-of-the-century span demolished at the end of the last war. It's a suspension bridge in the manner of the Golden Gate of San Francisco. Crossing this bridge towards Buda, the head-on view takes in the St. Gellért monument high on the hillside, above a garden and manmade waterfall. The Buda-bound traffic disgorges onto a complicated system of viaducts and underpasses. In the parkland interspersed among all these engineering projects you may notice another Turkish bath, Rácz fürdő, across the road from the north edge of Gellért Hill. A dome from the Turkish era still covers one bathing pool.

This is the old Tabán district of Buda, where the ferrymen and other noted characters used to live. Only a few houses are left. One of them, a restored Louis XVI mansion at 1–3 Apród utca, was the birthplace of Professor Ignác Semmelweis (1818–65). He discovered the cause of puerperal fever, greatly improving world life-expectancy tables. The upper floor of the building now shelters the **Semmelweis Museum of the History of Medicine** (*Semmelweis Orvostörténeti Múzeum*). Multilingual guides in white smocks

2 Hercules Villa
3 Roman Camp Museum
4 Military Amphitheatre
5 Ski-lift
6 Children's Railway
7 Cog Railway
8 Sas-hegy Nature Reserve

CSILLAGHEGY

RÁKOSPALOTA

ÚJPEST

RÓMAIFÜRDŐ

CINKOTA

ÁRPÁDFÖLD

RÁKOSSZENTMIHÁLY

SASHALOM

MÁTYÁSFÖLD

RÁKOSKERESZTÚR

RÁKOSHEGY

ÚJPALOTA

PESTÚJHELY

ANGYALFÖLD

ZUGLÓ

KŐBÁNYA

PESTLŐRINC

KISPEST

PESTERZSÉBET

Aquincum

Tabororos Múzeum

Hercules villa

ÓBUDA

Katonai amfiteátrum

Margit sziget

Gellért-hegy

KELENFÖLD

CSEPEL

ALBERTFALVA

BUDAFOK

PASARÉT

RÓZSADOMB

Sas-hegy

SASAD

Sas-hegy
Természetvédelmi
Terület

HŰVÖSVÖLGY

Hármashatár-hegy

PESTHIDEGKÚT

Solymár

Bécsi út

Libegő

János-hegy

Svábhegy

Fogaskerekű vasút

Szabadság-hegy

Gyermek-vasút

Budakeszi

BUDAÖRS

Törökbálint

BUDAPEST AND THE HILLS

VIENNA

BALATON

point out gruesome ancient surgical instruments and anatomical models, and there are enlightening exhibits illustrating the path of medicine from witch doctors' amulets to modern times.

Northward from the museum, the riverside area has a character of its own. The hillside facing the Danube, leading up to the Royal Palace, is adorned with arcades, terraces, ceremonial staircases and neo-Classical statues. The architect of this scheme, Miklós Ybl (1814–91), who also designed the Basilica, the Opera House and other monumental buildings, is himself the subject of a monument near the river.

The often-clogged traffic roundabout at the Buda end of the Chain Bridge occupies Clark Ádám tér, a square named, in back-to-front Hungarian style, in memory of a Scottish engineer called Adam Clark. He oversaw construction of the bridge, a wonder of

19th-century technology. The man who designed it, William Tierney Clark, an English engineer, was no kin to Adam Clark. The **Széchenyi Lánchíd** (Chain Bridge), the first across the Danube, was opened to traffic in 1849, blown up by German sappers towards the end of the last war, but soon rebuilt.

Straight ahead of the bridge, Adam Clark constructed a tunnel beneath the Castle District plateau. Because of the juxtaposition of bridge and tunnel, a standard little joke in Budapest claims the bridge is pulled into the tunnel when it rains, so the chains don't rust. Left of the tunnel is the terminus of the vintage train that runs uphill to the Castle District.

The street north from Clark Ádám tér, Fő utca (meaning Main Street), follows the original Roman route linking the Danube military outposts. About half a mile north of the Chain Bridge, at **Batthyány tér,** the metro, bus and tram systems meet the suburban railway; there's a boat station at this important junction, too. This is the best place in town for an all-encompassing view of the Hungarian Houses of Parliament, directly across the river. The effect is rather like a mutation of London's parliament building, with the Danube substituted for the Thames.

The terminal of the Vienna stagecoach used to be right around the corner and, on the west side of Batthyány tér, an 18th-century hostelry was famous. The emperor and many dignitaries stayed at the White

The towers of Inner City Parish Church, begun in the 12th-century, rise alongside Elizabeth Bridge. **43**

Cross Inn, a venue for carnival balls and festivities of the district, called Víziváros (Watertown). The palatial two-storey **Rococo building** has been preserved, but its role has changed a bit; now it's a nightclub.

Szent Anna templom (St. Anne's Church), on the south side of the square, reveals Italian influences on Hungarian architecture of the mid-18th century. Tall twin towers top the Baroque façade, embellished with statues. The oval-domed interior contains more 18th-century statues and frescoes.

Farther north along Fő utca, a crescent surmounts the dome of a Turkish bath established in the 16th century. **Király fürdő** (Király Baths), a rambling green stone building, expanded over the centuries as Baroque and neo-Classical additions were made. The authentic Turkish section has survived, with an octagonal bathing pool under the largest of the domes. After the expulsion of the Turks the royal treasurer took possession of the baths, but in the 19th century they were owned by a family called König. The name means "king" in German, which is *király* in Hungarian, hence the modern title.

An offbeat attraction of this district, at 20 Bem József utca, is a 19th-century iron foundry, now operated as a museum *(Öntödei Múzeum)*. A statue honours the originator of the enterprise, a Swiss industrialist named Abraham Ganz. The factory maintained production from 1845 all the way to 1964 and was noted for its tramwheels. Museum exhibits follow the evolution of technology from the Iron Age to the 20th century and include some handsome examples of the founder's art—iron stoves, statues, ships' propellers and bells.

The main street of this area, Margit körút curves gradually towards the Danube and finally leads its tram, bus and car traffic across Margit híd (Margaret Bridge). This connects with the southern tip of Margaret Island, then deflects from the conventional arrow-straight trajectory. Thus from certain angles the bridge appears to end in mid-air. But it really does reach Pest. The big white post-war building at the bridgehead, in an architectural style reminiscent of government offices in Washington, D.C., was the Socialist Worker's Party headquarters. In Budapest slang the building is called the White House.

Back in Buda, hilly streets zigzag north-westward from the bridge approaches up to the **Gül Baba türbéje** (tomb). This meticulously preserved relic of the Turkish era stands at 14 Mecset utca. The mausoleum was built in the middle of the 16th century by order of the pasha of Buda. It covered the grave of Gül Baba, a well-known dervish whose funeral the sultan himself attended. After the expulsion of the Turks, the octagonal building was used for a time as a Jesuit chapel. Restoration in recent years has been enhanced by a gift of art works from the Turkish government.

Óbuda

Heavy traffic rumbles along Pacsirtamező utca, the principal artery leading out of Budapest to the north. At its intersection with Nagyszombat utca, the road travels alongside the almost flattened but instantly identifiable remains of a Roman amphitheatre, one of the biggest outside Italy. This is part of Aquincum, capital of the Roman province of Lower Pannonia, later called Óbuda (Old Buda).

The **Military Amphitheatre** (*Katonai Amfiteátrum*) as it is known to distinguish it from a smaller one a couple of miles to the north, dates from the 2nd century. Here, gladiators performed for the amusement of the Roman legionaries who guarded this far frontier. Up to 16,000 spectators could be packed in when the contest drew a full house. The events took place on an elliptical arena more than 140 yards long. After the fall of the empire, a fortress was built on the site, and in later centuries houses took over the floor of the all-but-forgotten stadium. The ruins were excavated and very partially restored starting in the 1930s.

At 63 Pacsirtamező utca, workmen building an apartment block came upon the remains of public buildings from the Roman era. They constructed the new house around the "digs" which now form part of the basement. The prize discovery was a hunting mural of an archer on horseback, a work of considerable grace. Details of the comprehensive heating and plumbing system can also be seen, and some artefacts found on the spot are displayed in this historic hideaway, known as the **Roman Camp Museum** (*Római Tábor Múzeum*).

Elsewhere in Óbuda, the ruins of a large bathing installation built for the Roman

Two thousand years on, a Roman fresco decorates a wall in Óbuda.

legion have been uncovered and protected in what is now the basement of a house at 3 Flórián tér. (The museum entrance is around the corner in Kórház utca.) The complexities of the baths, central heating system and all, intrigue visitors. Archaeologists of the distant future may be fascinated by the area on the northwest side of Flórián tér, the site of Budapest's first major multistorey shopping centre.

The remains of a grand Roman residence known as **Hercules Villa** lie in and around a modern school at 21 Meggyfa utca. The villa contained the finest mosaic floors found in all Pannonia. The central panel of the most famous scene, said to portray Hercules and his wife Deianira, was created out of small squares of marble and basalt in the early 3rd century.

The most extensive of the Roman achievements to come to light in Budapest, the civil town of **Aquincum,** accommodated the artisans, merchants, priests and other non-military personel attached to the legion. All the elements of a civilized town are here, from running water to central heating. The foundations of villas, workshops and markets have been uncovered. Clumps of poplars enliven the expanse of walls, knee-high to chest-high, and a few columns have been reconstructed to help the imagination. More has yet to be unearthed.

The site extends just east of Szentendrei út, the highway which, as route 11, continues on to the town of Szentendre. If you're travelling on the suburban railway *(HÉV)*, get off at the Aquincum stop and cross the highway, then go under the railway bridge. An ordinary tram ticket suffices.

At the entrance to the excavations, you can buy an inexpensive leaflet including a map of the civil town pointing out such sights as the Sanctuary of the Goddess Fortuna Augusta and the baths with their cold-, tepid- and hot-water pools. Even with a map you could lose your way in the far-flung ruins.

An imitation Roman building on the site houses a **museum** of the statues, pots, glassware, coins, tools and objects of everyday Roman life found in the ground here. Surrounding the museum on three sides, the **lapidarium** overflows with sarcophagi, columns and stone-carvings. The original inscriptions, of course, are all in Latin, posing yet another linguistic challenge to the foreign visitor.

Black and Blue

The Danube, blue in song only, originates in the Black Forest and empties into the Black Sea. At 1,776 miles from source to mouth, the Danube is Europe's second-longest river (after the Volga). It's longer than the Orinoco, the Irawaddy or the Rhine. Flowing through eight countries, the Danube goes under six different names; the Hungarians call it the Duna.

Inside Budapest the river, between 300 and 500 yards wide, is now spanned by eight bridges. For centuries, however, the only way to get from Buda to Pest was by ferry. Pontoon bridges were attempted but they were inevitably swept away by floods or rampaging ice floes.

In the early 19th century Count István Széchenyi rallied support for the first permanent bridge. The resulting Chain Bridge *(Lánchid)* was designed by British engineers and finally linked Buda and Pest in 1849.

Margaret Island

The Roman empire's élite escaped the cares of the day on this island halfway between Aquincum and Pest. In later eras, princes and plutocrats took refuge in the peace and quiet of mid-Danube. Margaret Island still serves as a sanctuary, but for more than a century the ordinary citizens of Budapest have been allowed to enjoy it. Within sight of the busiest parts of town, the feather-shaped, forested island is insulated from all the noise and bustle. You couldn't dream of a happier project.

Margaret Island is $1\frac{1}{2}$ miles long and a few hundred yards wide at the middle. With its ageless woods, vivid flowerbeds and varied recreational facilities, it's a favourite spot for sports, amusements or just meditating. The island has been kept virtually free of motor traffic. Except for summer Sundays, the birds often have the place to themselves.

The southern end of the island is joined to "mainland" Buda and Pest by Margaret Bridge, a modern replacement for the original 19th-century span. It was destroyed in 1944, with needless loss of life, when German demolition charges went off prematurely.

Near the southern tip of the island, a tall bronze monument—shaped like a Hungarian version of yin and yang—commemorates the centenary of the unification of Buda and Pest. Margaret Island, equidistant between the two, is the obvious place for it.

The sports establishments on the island include Youth Stadium (Ifjúsági stadion), the National Sports Swimming Complex (Hajós Alfréd-uszoda) and the huge Palatinus Outdoor Public Swimming Complex (Palatinus strand). The Palatinus installation, with cold- and warm-water pools, can hold 20,000 swimmers and sunbathers. There's even an artificial wavemaker.

Alongside the turn-of-the-century water tower, an open-air theatre (Szabadtéri Színpad) presents concerts, opera and ballet performances in the summer. The theatre's immense stage is conducive to lavish sets and productions. The park has a separate open-air cinema.

Near the outdoor theatre, you can wander through the ruins of a **Dominican Convent** (Domonkos kolostor romjai) founded by the 13th-century Hungarian King Béla IV. He

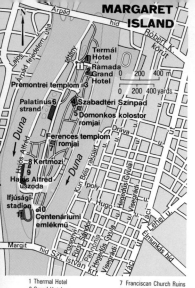

1 Thermal Hotel
2 Grand Hotel
3 Premonstratensian Chapel Ruins
4 Open-air Theatre
5 Dominican Convent Ruins
6 Palatinus Swimming Complex
7 Franciscan Church Ruins
8 Open-air Cinema
9 National Sports Swimming Complex
10 Centennial Monument
11 Youth Stadium
[i] Tourist Information

stratensian Chapel *(Premontrei templom)*, a 20th-century reconstruction of a 12th-century church. The bell in the tower is said to be the oldest in Hungary; it survived the Turkish demolition of the church because it was buried nearby. The history of the reconstituted St. Michael's Church is spelled out on signs on the front of the building—in Latin, English, German, French, Polish, Russian and Hungarian.

The woods near the chapel are thickly populated with statues and busts of Hungary's foremost writers and artists.

In 1866 deep drilling operations on Margaret Island hit a gusher—scalding hot mineral water. Soon the island became well-known as a therapeutic spa for sufferers from an ample range of ailments, from rheumatism to nervous disorders. Two large spa hotels have been set up at the north end of the island, accessible via Árpád Bridge. Taking advantage of the water and the prize location are the century-old Grand Hotel and, under the same management (Ramada), the even bigger modern Thermal Hotel. People taking the cure are tempted by all manner of distractions on the premises—restaurants, cafés, bars and a nightclub.

enrolled his daughter in the convent when she was 11 years old, and she never left. Her burial place is marked by a marble plaque. She was called Princess (later Saint) Margaret; the island is named after her.

Another archaeological site on the island reveals the remains of a 13th-century Franciscan church *(Ferences templom romjai)* and monastery.
50 And then there is the **Premon-**

Pest

The bulk of modern Budapest lies to the east of the Danube in what, until little more than a century ago, was the autonomous city of Pest. The government buildings, big stores, museums and nightlife are concentrated in Pest. There are no hills to climb on this side of the river, but plenty of worthwhile sights to see along busy streets and imposing boulevards.

From the viewpoint of a Roman general defending Buda and western civilization, the Pest side of the river meant nothing but trouble. He could only stare out at the flatlands—badlands—and wonder when the barbarians would try to ford the Danube. In A.D. 294, to make it harder for any invaders to launch an amphibious attack, the Romans established an outpost on the left bank. They called it Contra-Aquincum, and it forms the very core of innermost Pest.

The medieval town grew around the Roman beachhead, evolving into a long, narrow strip, with the Danube to the west and defensive walls on the other sides. The Kiskörút, or inner boulevard of Pest (see p. 65), follows the contours of those city walls—fragments of which are still to be seen. The enclosed area—District V of modern Budapest—contains a stimulating sample of what's best in Pest: historic monuments, riverside hotels and promenades, and shopping the locals claim is the nearest thing to Paris.

The oldest church—indeed, the oldest surviving structure —in all of Pest is **Belvárosi templom** (Inner City Parish Church). It's hemmed in alongside the elevated approach road to Elizabeth Bridge. Viewed from the front it appears to be contemporary with several other nearby churches. The twin Baroque towers and the façade, with nicely balanced windows, date from the early 18th century and were restored twice thereafter. But the church was founded in the 12th century. Parts of the original Romanesque construction can be discerned, but these elements blend into the Gothic with little more than a ripple in the walls and roof. The Turks who occupied Budapest in the 16th century turned the church into a mosque and carved a *mihrab* (prayer niche) on the Mecca side of the chancel wall.

The plaza alongside the church, Március 15. tér, takes **51**

1	Ifjúsagi Stadion
2	Lukács Baths
3	Gül Baba Tomb
4	Zoo
5	Széchenyi Baths
6	Museum of Fine Arts
7	Art Gallery
8	Castle of Vajdahunyad
9	Transport Museum
10	Iron Foundry Museum
11	Király Baths
12	Western Railway Ststion
13	Ethnographic Museum
14	Parliament
15	Museum of East Asian Art
16	Museum of Chinese Art
17	St. Anne's Church
18	State Opera House
19	St. Stephen's Basilica
20	Eastern Railway Station
21	Underground Railway Museum
22	Lutheran Museum
23	Jewish Religious and Historical Museum
24	City Hall
25	Post Office
26	Semmelweis museum
27	Inner City Parish Church
28	Franciscan Church
29	University
30	Hungarian National Museum
31	University Church
32	St. Gellért Monument
33	Rudas Baths
34	Citadel
35	Liberation Monument
36	Applied Arts Museum

Museums   Baths

Churches   i Tourist Information

Tourist Sights   Metro

Note that many street names in Budapest,
and throughout Hungary, are being changed.
It is advisable to get the latest street map
from the tourist office, see p.122.

its name from the day in March 1848 when the revolution for Hungarian independence broke out in Pest. A sunken park created around the excavations of **Contra-Aquincum** catches the spring sunshine and excludes winter winds. Here children play amid the much-restored rockpile representing the 3rd-century Roman outpost. Above stands a modern fountain with statues symbolizing Roman legionaries in action.

An ornate two-storey structure, termed the only surviving Baroque mansion in Pest, lies just up the street in Pesti Barnabás utca. Notice the marker next to the doorway—a sculpted finger pointing to the level the Danube attained during the flood of 1838. A restaurant has operated in this building for 150 years.

Cobbled centrepiece of an expansive pedestrian zone, **Váci utca** is the Bond Street of Budapest. The narrow street

tempts shoppers with the last word in Hungarian fashions, as well as art works, cosmetics, furnishings, jewellery and handicrafts. Several large bookstores along Váci utca sell Hungarian-published books in foreign languages. Also in the street are the offices of the major airlines and the high-rise premises of the International Trade Centre and Central European International Bank. With a variety of cafés, clubs and restaurants, the Taverna Hotel and entertainment complex is a new Váci utca attraction.

Lift your eyes above shop-window level and study some of the turn-of-the-century buildings on this street. They include intriguing experiments in modern architecture, notable for their unusual angles, window shapes and sculptural additions. An illuminated sign reading Pesti Színház (Pest Theatre) hangs over the street. In the entrance of the theatre **55** a plaque observes that Franz Liszt made his Pest debut as a pianist here at age 12.

Váci utca runs into the busy yet relaxed square named after Mihály Vörösmarty, a nationalistic poet and dramatist of the 19th century. (Cars are now banned here.) Not many pastry shops become national monuments, but the establishment on the north side of the square, the Gerbeaud, certainly qualifies. It used to be owned by the Gerbeaud family of Swiss confectioners; enthusiasts say the quality of the cakes and strudel hasn't deviated since the old days. The sumptuous interior with its high-ceilinged halls has been preserved, and in pleasant weather the terrace is a favourite spot for people-watching calorie-collectors.

A concert hall has stood on the site of the newly refurbished **Vigadó** since 1832, but not without a couple of long, involuntary intermissions. The first hall was destroyed in the shelling of the 1848 revolution, the second in the closing stage of World War II. In 1980 an acoustically perfect auditorium was opened; it's concealed behind the restored façade of mid-19th-century Hungarian-Oriental-Moorish style. The **56** list of conductors and performers who appeared in the old Vigadó sums up the history of 150 years of European music: Liszt, Brahms, Wagner, Bartók, Prokofiev, Rubinstein, Heifetz, Casals, Gigli, Björling, von Karajan....

Cruise boats for Budapest sightseeing tours and trips to the Danube Bend leave from the embarkation point at Vigadó tér. In the square between the river and the concert hall stands a marble obelisk engraved simply "1945" and, in Russian and Hungarian, "Glory to the Soviet hero-liberators".

Inland again, **Martinelli tér,** the site of an outdoor market in the 18th century, offers room enough to step back and admire the architecture. The seven-storey building at No. 5 is considered one of Europe's best examples of pre-modern design. Ceramic tiles ranged in horizontal bands decorate the upper floors in a scheme that was considered revolutionary when the house was completed in 1912. An Art Nouveau building two doors down also catches the eye. It's notable for the mosaic fantasy at roofline, a patriotic and religious scene surrounded by "3-D" embellishments. The former Servite Church on the square was built in Baroque style in the early 18th-century. Martinelli tér also boasts a Budapest rarity: a high-rise parking garage with room for 300 cars.

Just off the square, Budapest's **City Hall** *(Főváros Főpolgarmesteri Hivatal)* fills an entire street. The imposing Baroque building served as a home for Hungarian veterans disabled in the fighting against the Turks. The 19th-century neo-Classical Pest County Hall *(Pest megyei Önkormányzati Hivatal)* lies just beyond a bend in the same street.

If you're caught in the rain in this part of town, you can duck into the **Paris Arcade** *(Párisi udvar)* for some indoor window-shopping. This early 20th-century project sports a high vaulted ceiling and some indescribably quaint architectural touches. Even the jumbo telephone kiosks were specially designed.

A pedestrians-only shopping street, **Kígyó utca,** runs between Váci utca and the heavy traffic of Ferenciek tere (Franciscan Square). Across all the lanes of cars and buses (but accessible only by pedestrian subway), you can see the refined Baroque lines of a Franciscan church topped by an unexpected neo-Gothic spire. On this site stood a 13th-century church which became a mosque under Turkish rule. Set into the wall of the church, on the Kossuth Lajos utca elevation, is another reminder of the 1838 flood: a sculptural tribute to Baron Miklós Wesselényi, shown standing in a rowboat rescuing people from their rooftops.

A large shop next door to the church, in Ferenciek tere, specializes in religious vestments, candles, statues and icons.

Károlyi Mihály utca contains some distinguished institutions: the Library of the Eötvös Loránd University of Arts and Sciences, the Petőfi Literary Museum, and the university faculties of political science and law (on Egyetem tér). Take a look, too, at **University Church** *(Egyetemi templom)* just off the square in Eötvös Loránd utca. It was built in the 18th century by the Order of St. Paul, the only monastic body of Hungarian origin. The monks themselves fashioned some of the richest wood-carvings inside the church—the stalls, the choir and the Baroque organ, which delights the eyes as much as the ears. The church, bigger within than seems likely from the street, has two graceful towers with bulbous spires in the Budapest style.

In this part of Pest, near the inner boulevard, you stand the best chance of coming upon traces of the medieval city wall. In many cases houses have been built around parts of the wall, so you have to peer into courtyards to find the high crenellated form of Pest's first defences. Some addresses for the archaeological sightseer: 21 Múzeum körút, 28 Magyar utca, 13 Királyi Pál utca, 17 and 19 Bástya utca and 16 Vámház körút.

This façade in Martinelli tér is one of Budapest's outstanding examples of Art Nouveau design.

From Erzsébet Square

An attractive fountain graces Erzsébet tér, one of the busiest squares of Budapest. The fountain, called the Danubius, is crowned by a bearded man symbolizing the Danube. Three female figures below represent tributaries of the mighty river, the Tisza, the

Dráva and the Száva. After the war a sprawling inter-city coach terminal was built on the square, bringing bustle and diesel fumes to the area.

Deák tér, only a few steps away, straddles all three metro lines. No more apt place could have been chosen for an **Underground Railway Museum** *(Földalatti Vasúti Múzeum);* it is even situated below ground. (The museum entrance is in the pedestrian underpass beneath Tanács Körút.) On view are antiquated and modern metro cars and equipment. Budapest's original underground line, inaugurated in 1896, was the first in continental Europe. It's still in operation, from Vörösmarty tér to Mexikói út, beyond City Park.

Above ground, a new museum adjoins the neo-Classical Evangelical Church building in Deák tér. The National Lutheran Museum *(Evangélikus Országos Múzeum)* contains a valuable collection of old bibles and chalices, plus documents concerning distinguished Protestant statesmen who strongly influenced the history of predominantly Catholic Hungary. The gigantic statue of Martin Luther in the courtyard next door perpetuates the memory of the Reformation leader.

59

Anker Palace, an overpowering building topped by two domes and a heavy pyramidal roof, dominates the far side of Deák tér. This one-time insurance company headquarters, adorned with a jumble of classical elements, was one of the few stuctures in Budapest to be left unscathed by the bombs and shells of World War II.

The main avenue leading north, Bajcsy-Zsilinszky út, named after a wartime resistance leader executed in 1944, continues the inner boulevard system. Many of the houses along here are proud examples of the novelties introduced into Budapest architecture at the turn of the century.

The biggest church in Budapest backs onto the boulevard. Construction of the **Basilica** dragged on from 1851 to 1905, long enough to employ three different architects, who chose neo-Classical, Eclectic and neo-Renaissance themes. The formal name of the church is St. Stephen's Parish Church *(Szent István templom)*, but everyone calls it the Basilica, even though this is an architecturally inaccurate title. King (St.) Stephen I appears in sculptured form above the main portal and on the altar. The dome, now 315 feet high, collapsed in 1868 and needed

re-doing. The Basilica is big enough to hold more than 8,000 worshippers, and often does.

Due west of the Basilica, at the Pest end of the Chain Bridge, **Roosevelt tér** honours the wartime U.S. president. (The plaque, in what might be an attempt at a compromise between Hungarian and American usages, identifies him as Delano Franklin Roosevelt.) The building directly facing the bridge, embellished to the last Art Nouveau detail, is the turn-of-the-century Gresham Palace. On the north side of the square stands the 19th-century neo-Renaissance home of the Hungarian Academy of Sciences. The statue in front depicts Count István Széchenyi (1791–1860), founder of the Academy and the dynamo behind the audacious Chain Bridge project. This first permanent link between the eastern and western halves of Hungary is now called Széchenyi Lánchíd, permanently linking the count's name with his brainchild.

Recent construction along the embankment south of

Inside the Parliament building, seen, below, from Szabadság tér.

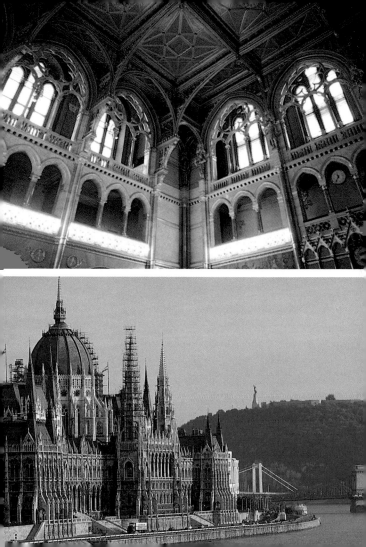

Roosevelt tér has restored the area to its pre-war position as a centre of luxury hotels. The first of them was the Duna Intercontinental, followed by the Forum Hotel Budapest and the Atrium Hotel. All were built under international agreements. From these hotels, the view across the Danube is priceless: the Citadel, the sprawling palace, the Fishermen's Bastion and the high-flying spire of Matthias Church.

Szabadság tér (Freedom Square), a vast expanse of shade trees and lawns, has its share of monuments, too, including another obelisk dedicated to Soviet soldiers. Official buildings, most of them ostentatious, surround the square. The former Stock Exchange, a showy Eclectic

Kálvin tér preserves a memento of Budapest's medieval city wall.

structure, now belongs to Hungarian Television; the Hungarian National Bank headquarters opposite is the work of the same architect.

The **Houses of Parliament** *(Országház)* were built to symbolize the grandeur of the Austro-Hungarian empire. In its day the building was called the biggest in the world. The architect, Imre Steindl (1839–1902), may have had the British parliament on his mind; in any case, the neo-Gothic arches and turrets of Hungary's riverside legislature inevitably remind one of the Westminster style. Out of character, however, is the great dome. At 315 feet, it's the same height as that of the Basilica, putting church and state on an equal plane.

Individual tourists are not admitted to the building, but group excursions are run by the various tour agencies when parliament is not in session. Guides point out the many works of art, the grandiose central stairway where the red carpet is always rolled out, and just off the former Chamber of Deputies, the Victorian brass cigar-park with numbered perches for the convenience of caucusing lawmakers who might have wanted to nip inside just long enough to vote.

Tourists are escorted into the Assembly Chamber and seated at the desks of members to be lectured on how the National Assembly is elected and does its work. In recent years the rubber-stamp sessions have been replaced by meaningful debates and historic votes.

Across Kossuth Lajos tér **63**

Naive painting celebrates life in the Hungarian countryside.

from the Parliament building, the **Ethnographic Museum** *(Néprajzi Múzeum)* occupies an 1890s building originally meant to be the seat of the Supreme Court (hence the statue of Justice on the façade). The main hall, with its vaulted, frescoed ceiling, is vast enough to serve as a railway station and pompous enough for a royal palace. On permanent display are examples of old-time Hungarian peasant art and culture: textiles, clothing, implements, ceramics and religious icons. An unusual and helpful feature of the museum is that explanations are supplied in English as well as Hungarian.

Beyond the Inner City

Breaking out from the inner city, there are no more ancient monuments—indeed, few buildings more than 150 years old. But the charm of the Pest which expanded so confidently in the 19th and early 20th centuries is hard to resist. Here are the majestic boulevards, the ingeniously decorated apartment blocks, the grand public buildings, the theatres and cafés.

The Little Boulevard (Kiskörút) follows the path of the medieval city wall. The first section starts at the Pest end of Liberty Bridge; it goes by the name of Vámház Körút. The road is hectic and businesslike, and there is little that holds any interest for sightseers. The exception (at No. 1–3) is a vast, old-fashioned covered market with a ceiling six stories above the floor, that used to be Budapest's central market, brimming with local colour and exotic smells. But in the early 1990s the old structure was found to be unsafe, and reconstruction is expected to take a great deal of time.

At Kálvin tér the boulevard veers northward along the trajectory of the city wall. The unaffected lines of an early 19th-century Calvinist church stand out, a reminder of the days when this was a quiet, almost rural, crossroads. Kálvin tér has since evolved into one of Budapest's biggest and busiest traffic intersections.

From here the boulevard is called Múzeum körút. It's dominated by the neo-Classical bulk of the **Hungarian National Museum** (*Magyar Nemzeti Múzeum*). This impressive building, with Corinthian columns and richly sculptured tympanum, stands back in its own sizable garden. Inside, amid monumental architectural and ornamental details, the whole story of Hungary unfolds. On display are prehistoric remains and ancient jewels and tools, longbows, locks and keys. From the Turkish era a 17th-century tent is all decked out with carpets on the floor and walls. The 19th-century exhibits range from army uniforms to a piano owned by Liszt, and by Beethoven before him.

For Hungarian visitors, though, there's no argument about which exhibit is the stellar attraction: the Hungarian **royal regalia.** They were returned to Budapest in 1978 after more than three decades in custody in the United States as spoils of war (including a spell in Fort Knox). The crown, attributed to St. Stephen, the great 11th-century king, has more meaning than most. In Hungary it is a powerful symbol of national pride. Also on show are the 11th-century coronation robes, the oriental-style sceptre, the 14th-century gilded orb, and a 16th-century replacement for a ceremonial sword. All are cherished as a supreme national treasure, even more so because of their post-war odyssey.

Beyond the university buildings, the boulevard crosses busy Rákóczi út (named after an 18th-century prince). This is the main east-west avenue of Budapest, and a major shopping street for goods ranging from shoes and antiques to TV sets. Rákóczi út runs straight towards the Eastern Railway Station *(Keleti pályaudvar)* but swerves at the last moment to create a modern plaza with a sunken promenade. The design of the station has been described as Eclectic in style. Statues of James Watt, inventor of the steam engine, and George Stephenson, of the steam locomotive, stand in niches of honour on the façade.

A final curiosity just off the inner boulevard at 2–8 Dohány utca: a mid-19th-century synagogue built in a striking Byzantine-Moorish style. This is the biggest of about 30 synagogues still operating in Budapest. Next door, the **Jewish Religious and Historical Collection** *(Zsidó Múzeum)* contains relics and works of art reflecting many centuries of Jewish life and death in Hungary. Among the exhibits: a 3rd-century gravestone, exquisite medieval prayerbooks and chilling documents on the fate of the Budapest ghetto in World War II.

The Nagykörút

The Great Boulevard *(Nagykörút)* makes a leisurely semicircle about four miles long, embracing all of Pest from Margaret Bridge to Petőfi Bridge. From dawn to late night it's crowded with tram, bus and car traffic. Though it changes names five times, the boulevard has a rather consistent character—not exceptionally elegant, but full of enthusiasm. Enterprising city planners pushed the project to completion for the thousandth anniversary of the Hungarian nation in 1896. With its wide roadway and ornate architectural monuments, the boulevard remains a good idea. And they don't build domes and towers like those any more.

Just off Ferenc körút at 33–37 Üllői út, a building pulsating with architectural shocks houses the **Museum of Applied Arts** *(Iparművészeti Múzeum)*. The style of the brick-and-ceramic-tile palace can only be described as Fantasy Hungarian with strong eastern influences. Designed by Ödön Lechner and Gyula Pártos, it was opened in 1896. As for the exhibits, they tell a terse history of ceramics in China, Europe and, in particular, Hungary. Also on show are furniture, textiles, oriental

The Eastern Railway Station is a showy relic of the Steam Age.

rugs, metalwork, clocks and curios made by extremely talented Hungarian and foreign hands.

A museum of more specialized interest, just beyond the ring of Erzsébet körút, is the Philatelic Museum *(Bélyegmúzeum)* at 47 Hársfa utca.

All the stamps ever issued by Hungary can be viewed here, so there are gripping historical and human-interest themes.

The segments of the boulevard known as Teréz and Erzsébet körút have been a traditional centre of Budapest's cultural as well as commercial life. Along here are theatres, cinemas and, less obviously, publishing houses and the haunts of literary and artistic characters. At the boulevard's intersection with Dohány utca, **67** the **New York Café** looks just as it did when the 20th century was new. The café's astonishing neo-Baroque-Eclectic-Art Nouveau interior has been restored to its original gaudy glory. And once again it's a popular meeting place of actors, writers and nostalgia buffs.

Teréz körút finally runs out at Nyugati tér, site of the Western Railway Station *(Nyugati pályaudvar)*. With its high-flying steel framework and cast-iron pillars, this was an architectural sensation of the 1870s. The French firm that built it went on to even greater heights with a daring project in Paris, which became known as the Eiffel Tower.

Most Stately Avenue

Budapest's most attractive avenue, modelled after the Champs-Elysées in Paris, was a bold stroke of the 1870s. The city planners pushed it straight out from the Inner Boulevard to City Park, gradually widening the avenue along the way and pausing for breath only at a couple of spacious squares.

Its name is again Andrássy út, as it was before the communists changed it to the unpronounceable Népköztársaság útja, meaning People's Republic Avenue. (The People's Republic name never caught on though.) Originally, the harmoniously styled avenue was called Sugár út (Radial Avenue). And at one time it even bore Stalin's name. Under whatever title, the avenue has a roomy, patrician feeling. The buildings that line it blend nicely, yet almost every one has unique features —a fountain or statue in the courtyard, a mosaic or frieze on the façade, columns or arches...

The **Postal Museum** *(Posta-múzeum)* is tucked away in a large, formerly aristocratic edifice near the beginning of the avenue at 3 Andrássy út. Even if you can't understand the explanations, written in Hungarian only, you will appreciate the rarity of the ancient telephone switchboards, telegraph keys, postboxes, and the telephone of Franz Joseph I. On view is the prototype of a revolutionary telegraph transmitter, with the letters of the alphabet assigned to the keys of a piano; but the idea was ahead of its time and won little acclaim.

The **State Opera House** *(Állami Operaház)*, designed by Miklós Ybl, is the most admired piece of architecture on the avenue. Its Italianate style and restrained proportions fit in beautifully with the surroundings. Statues of 16 great opera composers stand high above the entrance; alongside the portico in positions of honour are sculptures of Franz Liszt and his less celebrated contemporary, Ferenc Erkel, composer of the Hungarian national anthem and director of the opera house when it opened in 1884.

The interior design, noted for its pleasing proportions, evinces a general air of great luxury within the bounds of taste. The auditorium, with its splendid four-tiered gallery, provides excellent acoustics. Opera is so popular in Budapest that a second, larger opera house, the Erkel Theatre, was built to ease the pressure for tickets.

Across the avenue from the opera house, in a late 19th-century palace, Hungary's best dancers study at the State Ballet Institute.

An area two or three streets away has suffered the nickname of **Budapest's Broadway.** With the highest concentration of theatres of any single neighbourhood in the capital, as well as the Moulin Rouge nightclub, it's a lively part of town.

The first of the avenue's main intersections, Nagykörút,

is a bustling place called Oktogon (formerly November 7 tér, commemorating the Bolshevik revolution). Farther from the centre of town the avenue takes another break at Kodály körönd (circle), named after the composer and educator Zoltán Kodály (1882–1967), who lived here. The curving façades of the buildings ranged around this square are embellished with classical figures and inlaid designs of endless variety.

As the avenue heads out of town, posh villas and mansions in garden settings predominate. Most are now embassies or government offices, but the house at 103 Andrássy út holds the **Museum of East Asian Art** *(Hopp Ferenc Kelet-ázsiai Múzeum).* Ferenc Hopp was an art collector who died in 1919, bequeathing his villa and his hoard of Asian art works to the state. Since then, other collections have been added, bringing the inventory to some 20,000 items. A related institution, the **Museum of Chinese Art** *(Kína Múzeum),* occupies another enviable villa in the same district, at 12 Gorkij fasor. It specializes in ancient Chinese sculpture, ceramics and handicrafts.

Andrássy út ends in an outburst of pomp at Heroes' **69**

Square *(Hősök tere),* a wide-open space generously endowed with winter winds. Here stand the statues of patriotic import that form the **Millenary Monument,** begun on the thousandth anniversary of the Magyar conquest. At the heart of the ensemble rises a 118-foot column supporting a winged figure. Around the pedestal, statues show seven tribal chiefs riding horses. The carved likenesses of historical figures starting with King Stephen I stand in a semicircular colonnade, and there are all the requisite allegorical works as well. In front of this, the stone tablet of the Hungarian War Memorial commemorates the heroes who died for national freedom and independence.

Facing each other across the expanse of Heroes' Square, two neo-Classical structures seem at first glance to be reflections of one another, and indeed they were designed by the same architect. The considerably larger building on the left (north) side is the **Museum of Fine Arts** *(Szépművészeti Múzeum),* an institution of international significance.

On view from ancient times are Egyptian statues and mummy cases, Greek and Roman sculpture and vases. (A note

about the Hungarian legends: I.E. 3–1 SZ. = 3rd–1st century B.C.; I.SZ. 3. SZ = 3rd century A.D.)

The museum's holdings of Old Masters, of which about 600 can be seen at any time, include many sublime works of the Italian Renaissance. An area of unexpected strength is the Spanish school, with seven El Grecos and an ample selection of works by Velázquez, Murillo, Zurbarán and Goya. Many other masters are represented, from Hans Memling and Bruegel the Elder to Frans Hals, Rembrandt and Vermeer. Another surprise is the trove of French Impressionists and Post-Impressionists: Monet, Pissarro, Renoir, Cezanne, Gauguin and others.

It's really something of a miracle that these treasures hang here at all. The museum was shot up during the war, and in 1944 the paintings were tossed into railway freight wagons for hasty evacuation to Germany. Yet, very soon after the end of hostilities, the whole precious cargo, with only a few minor losses, was returned.

Temporary exhibitions of

Nightlife runs the gamut from opera to spectacular floor-shows.

are normally held in the Art Gallery *(Mucsarnok)* designed in the form of a Greek temple, found on the far side of the square, but like many buildings in Budapest it is currently under restoration.

Not far from the gallery, Dózsa György út widens to form Procession Square *(Felvonulási tér)*. This used to be the scene of those patriotic parades with red flags, rousing bands, and party officials taking the salute.

The City Park
(Városliget)

Beyond the Millenary Monument and all the exaggerated formality sprawls a park where Hungarians can relax, stroll in the woods, spoil their children with ice-cream and cheap plastic toys, hire a rowing boat, even visit another museum.

The City Park, about 250 acres in area, began to evolve in the early 19th century. Most of the present amenities, such

One wing of the castle holds the Hungarian Agricultural Museum *(Magyar Mezőgazdasági Múzeum)*, which deals with the history of hunting, fishing and farming. There's also a simulated wine cellar displaying old wine presses and bottles; oddly, the place is heated even in summer to protect the exhibits.

In the palace courtyard stands a unique statue of a 13th-century personage known only as Anonymous. He was the royal scribe who wrote the first Hungarian chronicles. A suitably anonymous face peers from deep inside a monk's cowl.

Outside the palace area, another statue shows the American president George Washington looking over a little lake—so far from the Delaware River and the Potomac. It was erected in 1906 by Hungarian émigrés living in the United States.

Sculpted elephants stand guard at the elaborately decorated entrance to the **Zoo** *(Fővárosi Állatkert)*. Inside, some 4,000 live animals stand by to entertain visitors. Most of them are kept in traditional

as the artificial lake which reflects the turrets of a make-believe castle, were added during preparations for the Thousand-Year festivities of 1896.

The **Castle of Vajdahunyad** *(Vajdahunyad vára)* reproduces aspects of the fabulous castle of the Hunyadi family in Transylvania (in an area which became part of Romania). It was built as a prop for the Millenary Exhibition but proved so popular that it was reconstructed in permanent form.

cages, but there are some refreshing exceptions, such as a monkey island in a lake. A hot-house on the zoo grounds displays tropical flora along with some appropriate but unlovely fauna—serpents and crocodiles.

The zoo adjoins **Vidám Park** (Amusement Park), a standard roller-coaster and dodgem establishment. For the foreign tourist, its principal attraction is the chance to watch young Hungarians having fun.

Across the street lies the overblown triple-domed **Széchényi Baths,** considered one of Europe's largest medicinal bath complexes. In a spa city like Budapest, it is probably to be expected that piping-hot spring water should bubble under the city park. The Széchényi installation treats various physical disorders and provides its share of swimming pools.

Near the easternmost point of the park (at 26 Hermina út), some worthy old trains, planes, cars and motorcycles may be examined in the **Transport Museum** *(Közlekedési Múzeum).* The exhibits skim the history of transport from the days of sail to the space age. In the museum grounds, an antique railway dining car now serves as a restaurant.

Excursions

Danube Bend

North of Budapest, where the Danube changes its mind and abandons its easterly course for a southerly tack, stretches the beautiful region known straightforwardly as Dunakanyar, the Danube Bend. The river is at its most alluring here, the lush countryside delights, and the towns glow with historic charm.

Scarcely 12 miles upstream from Budapest, easily reached by car, bus or suburban railway, is the captivating town of **Szentendre.** Though the area has been inhabited since the Stone Age, the present character of Szentendre remains frozen in the 18th century: tidy, Baroque and painted all the colours of the rainbow.

Fö tér, the cobbled main square, so perfectly embodies the spirit of times past that the whole ensemble has been classified as a national historical monument. (In over 200 years, the only thing about the square that's changed is its name.) The cast-iron Rococo cross in the centre of the square was erected in 1763 by the Serbian businessmen of Szentendre. By then, Serbs fleeing Ottoman rule made up most of the population of the town, to which they brought their religion, art and architecture.

The towers of seven churches dominate the Szentendre skyline. The one on Fö tér, a mid-18th-century Baroque church with some Rococo details on the portal and belfry, is known as the **Greek church**; officially it's the Blagoveštenska Eastern Orthodox Church. Alongside, in what was a schoolhouse in the 18th century, the Ferenczy Museum displays art works of the Hungarian Impressionist Károly Ferenczy and his two children.

Other churches of more than routine interest in the town: the Catholic Parish Church, founded in the Middle Ages, with an ancient sundial on the wall; and the Belgrade Church, an 18th-century Greek Orthodox cathedral noted for a richly sculpted iconostasis. Around the corner is the entrance to the Collection of Serbian Ecclesiastical Art *(Szerb Egyháztörténeti gyűjtemény)*, where precious icons, carvings and manuscripts have been gathered together.

Of all the museums in this artists' town, the one dedicated to the 20th-century ceramic artist Margit Kovács draws the biggest crowds. Here you'll see attenuated sculptures of wide-eyed damsels and stooped tragic figures in an instantly recognizable style. Opposite the Catholic Parish Church, a smaller museum vibrates with the happy, warm colours of paintings by Béla Czóbel, a much-travelled Hungarian Impressionist who settled in Szentendre.

About 2 miles north-west of town, typical old houses transplanted from the countryside have been assembled at the **Open Air Village Museum** *(Szabadtéri Néprajzi Múzeum)*. With its 18th-century tim-

ber church and whitewashed thatch-roofed cottages—and not a TV antenna in sight—this simulated "village" provides an ideal setting for historical films, as several producers have noticed.

Upriver, where the Danube makes a hairpin bend, historic **Visegrád** is set in surpassingly scenic country, where verdant hills come down almost to the water's edge. The strategic importance of this potential bottleneck on the river has been evident since the 4th century, when the Romans built a fort here.

The most enterprising construction work, in the Middle Ages, transformed Visegrád into a proper regal city. The Angevin kings of Hungary built their **palace** here, each monarch adding new luxury and a few dozen more rooms to the 14th-century nucleus. But the palace fell into ruin during the Turkish occupation and its former splendour was all but forgotten until archaeologists started digging it up in the 1930s. Only part of the main building has been unearthed; to give a better idea of the whole, certain areas have been reconstructed (using obviously new materials to differentiate these sections from the original elements).

Among the most celebrated sights of the five-level structure: the superb **Hercules Fountain** (a rare vestige of Hungarian Renaissance architecture); the vaulted galleries

Ceramics by Margit Kovács reflect Szentendre's quiet beauty.

Itinerant beekeepers set up their hives all through the rolling countryside. Right: Lions' Well in Visegrád.

of the Court of Honour; and the restored Lions' Fountain. Up the hillside, the hexagonal tower popularly called the Tower of Solomon contains a museum displaying fragments and reconstructions of items from the palace. Finally, near the top of the hill are the ruins **78** of the **Citadel,** with spectacular

views of the mountains and the river.

From Budapest, Visegrád may be reached by bus, but an altogether more inviting way to go is by ferryboat or hydrofoil. The boats land right in front of the palace.

Esztergom, cathedral city and medieval capital of all Hungary, is about 30 miles from Budapest by road, but just across the river from Czechoslovakia. In this part of the Danube Bend the river it-

self becomes an international frontier. The ruins of a bridge which, until World War II, linked the two countries make a melancholy sight from the heights of Castle Hill.

The great domed **Basilica of Esztergom** *(Esztergomi Székesegyház)*, the biggest church in Hungary, stands on the site of an 11th-century house of worship. In 1823, shortly after construction began, Beethoven offered to conduct his *Missa Solemnis* for the consecration of the church. But the work went too slowly, and when the ceremony finally took place, in 1856, it was Liszt's *Esztergom Mass* that was performed.

The red-marble side chapel called the **Bakócz-kápolna,** a pure example of Italian Renaissance style, was built as a separate church in the early 16th century. It was moved stone by stone to the basilica in the 19th century and reassembled. Note the white marble altar sculpted by a Florentine master. The **treasury** contains Hungary's richest store of religious objects, including a cross of crystal from 9th-century Metz and the 15th-century Calvary of King Matthias.

Alongside the basilica the remains of a medieval **royal palace** have been excavated and, to an extent, restored. Among the highlights; St. Stephen's Hall, the frescoed Hall of Virtues with the signs of the zodiac on the great arch, and the 12th-century royal chapel.

Down at riverside, Esztergom's **Christian Museum** *(Keresztény Múzeum)* is rated the most important provincial collection in Hungary. It definitely comes up to world standards, especially in its supply of superb 14th- and 15th-century Italian paintings. Housed in the former Episcopal Palace, the museum is run by the Catholic Church and subsidized by the state. Elsewhere in the building are photographs of some of the approximately 170 churches built in Hungary since the end of World War II.

Take time to stroll along the restful riverfront promenades nearby. And if you're in no hurry, you can take the boat on its effortless downstream journey back to Budapest.

Lake Balaton

Hungarians may be deprived of a seacoast but they take their solace in Lake Balaton, a freshwater haven surrounded by a little world of varied beauty: fertile plains and abrupt hills, orchards and vineyards, and villages with historic churches and whitewashed thatched cottages. At about 60 miles south-west of Budapest, Balaton lies within daytrip distance by car or coach (the journey can be made by motorway) or by express train.

Balaton is counted as Middle Europe's biggest lake, with an area of nearly 230 square miles. Yet its average depth is less than ten feet. In winter it quickly freezes from end to end. In summer the shallow water is subject to wind-driven waves; when a real storm blows up, the tiny sea gets so rough that even the ferryboats quit.

But for most of the summer the hot sun warms the calm lake nearly to air temperature, luring thousands into the swim. The mildly alkaline water is said to be positively healthful for bathing. The fish certainly thrive in it: about 40 species inhabit the lake. Balaton pike-perch *(fogas)* is often singled out as the tastiest of all.

Fishermen operate from shore, from boats and lounging on platforms protruding from the lake. Ice-fishing has been popular at Balaton since antiquity, when winter was the only season the catch could be preserved for sale in distant parts. Another commercial product comes from the lake—the reeds which grow along much of the shore. They make a good roofing material and have other practical uses.

More conventional agriculture flourishes all along the circumference of Lake Balaton, enhancing the appeal of the countryside with fruit trees, rippling expanses of wheat and vineyards. Some of Hungary's most popular wines originate here, so many, in fact, that a whole holiday could easily be devoted to studying them all.

Now for a brief survey of the points of greatest interest along the lake, taking them counter-clockwise from the eastern (Budapest) end. The only complication is the nomenclature; a couple of dozen of the towns have names beginning "Balaton", badly muddying the waters for new arrivals. BALATONAKARATTYA, for example, is the first town on Highway 71, the north shore road. Then comes BALATONKENESE, and so forth. Some

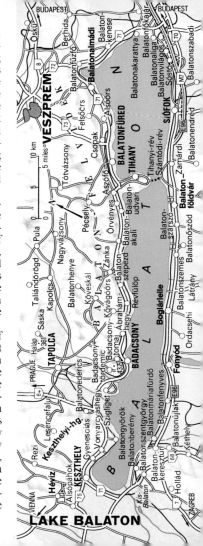

LAKE BALATON

of the names can barely be squeezed onto the road signs.

Balatonalmádi, a fast-growing resort town, claims to have the biggest, most modern beach on the north shore—"capacity 12,000". Parks, hotels and a complete shopping centre round out the picture.

The road leads about 8 miles farther west to **Balatonfüred,** a busy pleasure port with a long history as a spa. The local mineral water, at 1 forint per glass, is dispensed to the public from a pagoda-like well-head in the middle of Gyógy tér (Therapeutic Square). It's cool enough to be refreshing, but the taste—as if it had come out of a rusty pipe—hints at its medicinal properties. Between the square and the lake-front a large park shaded by tall plane and poplar trees is studded with

Visitors to Balaton take a break at an outdoor café with a view.

statues traditional and modern. In addition to its sanitoria and resort hotels, Balatonfüred has a campsite big enough for 3,000 people.

The **Tihany peninsula**, largely given over to a national park, protrudes to within about a mile of the south shore. Life here is a split-level affair—an ancient church stands on a precipice overlooking the port, and at intermediate altitudes there's a village and its independent lake.

Starting at the top: The **Abbey Church** *(Apátság)*, an 18th-century Baroque construction, rises above a crypt nearly a thousand years old. Here stands the tomb of King Andrew I, founder of this Benedictine abbey. In a country ravaged by so many invasions, the Romanesque crypt represents a rare survival from the earliest times of the Hungarian nation. King Andrew is also commemorated in a joltingly contemporary sculpture in front of the church—a stone figure wrapped in an aluminium cloak.

The streets and lanes along the upper reaches of **Tihany** town charm visitors. They're lined with thatch-roofed, stone cottages in traditional style.

At an altitude of more than 80 feet above Lake Balaton, the peninsula's Inner Lake (Belső-tó) yields tons of fish every year. Because it is so small—less than half a mile long—the green hills surrounding the little lake look like real mountains. To the south are the domes of defunct geysers.

Beyond Tihany the north coast traffic thins out, so travellers can relax and enjoy the views, vineyards and villages. The region of **Badacsony** produces notable wines on hill- **83** sides of volcanic soil. The volcanic past is evident at first sight of the astonishing conical green hills arrayed here. The black basalt slabs used to pave the back roads provide another clue to the violent birth of this land. The view up to the evocative Badacsony mountains is a high-spot of an excursion to Lake Balaton; so is the panorama from the top, with the vineyards sloping down to the lake in regimented rows. The next step is obvious: sample the local pride. The wine always tastes better when you're beside the vines.

The road moves inland after Badacsony, skirting the ancient village of SZIGLIGET, watched over by the moody remains of a medieval fortress.

At the western end of the lake, the town of **Keszthely** used to be owned lock, stock and barrel by one family— the Festetics. The 101-room **Festetics Palace** is one of Hungary's important Baroque monuments. Count György Festetics founded Europe's first agricultural school, now Keszthely's University of Agricultural Sciences, in 1797. He also amazed townspeople by building the *Phoenix*, the biggest ship seen on Balaton till then, a three-master powered with help from 24 oarsmen.

Keszthely's **Balaton Museum** surveys the lake from many viewpoints—geology, biology, history and ethnology.

The highway continues around the end of the lake to the first town on the south shore. This road and rail junction has a folk museum and the longest name: BALATON-SZENTGYÖRGY. To the west lies KIS-BALATON (Little Balaton), a national reserve noted for its rare birdlife.

When the highway (now route 7) finally comes in sight of the lake, Balaton's endless children's beach begins. All along the south shore the soft, white sandy bottom of the lake goes out seemingly to infinity before the water becomes deep enough to dive into. However, this is no problem for sailing, wind-surfing (board sailing) or simply paddling about. To protect the lake from pollution, motorboats (hence water-skiing) have been banned.

A volcanic hill with twin peaks hangs over **Fonyód,** the centre of a string of south coast resorts. Fonyód's harbour is one of Balaton's major maritime installations. Long after the bathers have packed up, fishermen stake out the unusually long pier and surrounding beaches.

At **Szántód** the great lake

is squeezed to its narrowest; the Tihany peninsula lies just across the way. This has always been a vital ferry station. Until 1928 oarsmen propelled the boats. Modern ferryboats make the crossing in less than ten minutes, but there's plenty of nautical excitement and fresh air. Although ferries and pleasure boats stop at many Balaton ports, the Szántód-to-Tihany route has the only car ferries on the lake.

The largest town on the south coast, **Siófok,** boasts a beach with room for tens of thousands of sunbathers and a harbour big enough to shelter all the ferries and cruise ships on the lake. A shady recreational park stretches east from the port and winds up in an ambitious new development of lake-front hotels. Around the harbour a lively assortment of cafés, bars, restaurants and entertainment facilities stand within easy reach.

In the 3rd century, Roman engineers built the first canal at Siófok to divert excess water from the lake. The Sió canal leads all the way from the harbour to the River Danube, down near the Southern border. The fastest, most direct way to return to Budapest from Siófok is via the M7 motorway.

What to Do

Some visitors come to Hungary with the most serious of intents. They potter about the Roman ruins or go birdwatching or sink into a therapeutic thermal bath. Other single-minded tourists sign up for hunting expeditions or horse-riding excursions. There are even package tours for bald men seeking the panacea of Hungarian hair-tonic and scalp treatment.

Most people, though, have broader horizons, and for them Budapest offers a wide variety of activities: excellent museums, pleasant boat trips, profitable shopping, plenty of sports, music of the highest standard, nightlife and renowned food and drink.

Shopping

Hungarian artisans, who provide the bulk of the best buys, offer some new lines as well as the dependable traditional designs. Other promising goods include low-priced books and records, along with foodstuffs —no big surprise in the land that invented paprika. In Hungarian shops and stores, the price tag tells the whole story. A VAT or sales tax of 25 per **85** cent, included in the price, is added to most goods and services (see pp. 111–112).

In addition to all the normal retail outlets, tourists can find a select range of Hungarian and imported goods in Intertourist and Utastourist shops (many of them in hotels), which accept hard currency only. Prices are usually listed in U.S. dollars, but almost all convertible currencies and credit cards are accepted. Two special shops in Budapest sell art, antiques and coins for foreign currency only. Keep your receipts in case of any questions at customs—on leaving Hungary or returning home.

Budapest's Best Buys

Antiques. Paintings, furniture, vases, jewellery, coins, leather-bound books, knick-knacks. The items for sale in hard-currency shops are suitable for export; in other shops, be sure to ask whether it's permitted to take the goods out of Hungary. (Precious art works may not leave.)

Books. Hungarian publishers produce very inexpensive picture books, travel guides and literary works written in or translated into English, French, German, Italian and **86** Spanish.

Carpets and rugs. Warm colours, rugged fabrics and harmonious designs distinguish Hungarian carpets and rugs of all sizes. They're advantageously priced—even the homespun, hand-knotted originals.

Ceramics. The best-known of the Hungarian factories, at Herend, near Lake Balaton, has been turning out porcelain plates, cups and vases since 1839. Other firms operate at Kalocsa and Pécs. Most of the designs available in Budapest shops are floral, but you'll even see imitation Chinese vases. Porcelain figurines of typical Hungarian characters are also popular.

Copper and brass. Plates, bowls, vases, ashtrays—and Turkish-style coffee sets.

Elixir. Some foreigners fly to Hungary just to buy bottles of the much-publicized tonic and suspected cure-all called Béres Csepp. Sold at shops of the Herbaria enterprise and at pharmacies; no prescription necessary.

Food products. Some items can be hand-carried out of the country: paprika in sachets or the ready-made sauce in tubes; strudel or cakes packed in sturdy boxes by the better confectioners' shops; and salami—the highest-quality Hungarian

At Tihany, Hungarian artisan produces distinctive hand-turned pottery.

spicy sausage, full-size or in more portable dimensions. (For export restrictions, see pp. 111–112.)

Furs. Small private workshops transform Hungarian and imported pelts into stylish winter hats and coats at very competitive prices.

Hair lotion. Thinning hair is said to be arrested by the use of Bánfi capillary lotion, another of Hungary's alleged miracle cures from the Herbaria shops, and at ordinary perfumeries as well. (If it works, forget the fur hat.)

Kitsch. If you're in the mood, buy a model of a Portuguese caravel with "Budapest" inscribed on the sail, or a simple air thermometer enshrined in a Rococo setting worthy of a reliquary—also marked "Budapest" as an afterthought.

Leather goods. Cowboy's whip and matching wine-bottle... from the Hungarian *puszta*. If time permits, you can have a pair of shoes made to fit and to last. Other interesting buys include leather gloves and wallets.

Linens. Embroidered table-cloths, napkins, doilies; each region, and virtually every village, has its own traditional designs.

Liqueurs and wine. The local apricot, cherry or plum brandy makes an inexpensive souvenir. Or take home a bottle of the best Tokay wine (some types come in gift packs).

Records and tapes. Aside from Liszt and Bartók, works galore. Hungarian performers have recorded many classic and modern pieces; also folk music, gypsy violins, Hungarian pop—all at low prices.

Rubik's puzzles. Having started with his Magic Cube, Professor Ernő Rubik then carried on with his daunting Snake, Magic Squares and Rubik Clock. They are so popular worldwide that the professor might well be the richest man in Hungary, had **88** he not moved to the U.S.A....

Shirts and blouses. Embroidered in primary colours, peasant-style blouses are a long-lasting reminder of Hungary. Men's shirts, off the rack or made to measure, include some bargains.

Silver. The workmanship of trays, pitchers, candelabra and smaller items is highly regarded, and the prices are considered extremely favourable.

Woodwork. Look for peasant-carved boxes big and small, bowls, walking sticks and chess sets.

Sports

For spectators or participants, Hungary offers a busy little world of sports. The strongest points involve horses and ball games. Aside from scuba divers and deep-sea fishermen, the only sportsmen likely to be disappointed are visiting golfers, who are completely out in the cold in Hungary.

Soccer, known by its Magyar name, *labdarúgás* (literally, kick-ball), draws the largest crowds. The big matches take place in Népstadion, the admired People's Stadium,

Lake Balaton anglers covet the fogas, *or giant pike-perch.*

with its graceful dimensions and full range of equipment. If you can't get a ticket, there are more than 3,200 other soccer grounds in the country.

Basketball, water-polo and **athletics**—fields in which Hungary often does well internationally—also attract sizable audiences in Budapest.

One of the pleasures of going to the **races** at the local tracks is looking at the spectators: workingmen, universal horse-players in Damon Runyon stripes and little old ladies who seem to be respected handicappers. Flat races *(galopp)* are run Sundays and Thursdays in summer, trotting races, year-round on Wednesdays and Saturdays. (Off-track betting at state lottery offices is also legal.)

Active Sports

To get closer to the horses, you can go for a ride—for an hour or on a week-long trek. There are numerous stables and **horse riding** schools just outside Budapest. In addition, package tours for horse-lovers, featuring friendly, lively Hungarian horses, start at many points in the country and last from five to ten days. IBUSZ issues a brochure, *Riding in Hungary,* with details. If you can't part with your horse, the agency says

Tourist shows recapture the romance of Hungary's puszta.

you can buy it and take it home.

Combine sports with sightseeing on a **cycling** tour to sites within a 30-mile radius of Budapest. Or pedal around the Balaton area for a week or more. Excursions by bike are another IBUSZ speciality.

On a hot summer's day, you may seek nothing more strenuous than a swim. Budapest has numerous **swimming** pools, including two elaborate installations on Margaret Island. But in this spa city, be sure to check the water temperature before you dive in!

For **sailing** and **wind-surfing,** the place to go is Lake Balaton or, closer to Budapest, the smaller Lake Velence. **Fishing** in the lakes or the Danube requires a permit from the Hungarian National Fishing Association (MOHOSZ, Budapest V. Október 6. u. 20). Try for bass, carp, catfish, pike and pike-perch.

Tennis is very popular in Hungary, but facilities for visitors are limited. And then there is **mini-golf,** played mostly around Lake Balaton.

For Children

Keeping children amused in Budapest is no big problem. The most obvious places to go are all in a row in the City Park: the zoo, the amusement park (with 50-year-old roller-coaster and modern rides) and the Budapest circus, one of Europe's best. Engrossing marionette shows by talented puppeteers take place in two special theatres, and outdoors in summer. The children's Railway, in the hills of Buda, employs children as station-masters and ticket-collectors. Or try a boat ride on the Danube, or the City Park lake.

An all-day excursion (aimed at adults) goes to the Hungarian *puszta* for, among other things, a show of horses which know some circus-style tricks, and a run-past of free horses, manes flying, on the prairie.

For a car-free, care-free outing, cross one of the bridges to Budapest's Margaret Island (Margitsziget), in the middle of the Danube. It's one big park, but there's also a tiny zoo, a Japanese garden, and bicycles for hire.

At Lake Balaton resorts, travel agencies organize children's parties, with story-teller, contests, children's songs, snacks and gifts.

Nightlife

Budapest has all the wholesome attractions you'd expect—heavily subsidized theatre, music and folklore—plus a few hedonistic surprises. Evenings are never boring.

Theatrical life is extremely active: on average, several new productions are premièred each week in Hungary. The language poses a problem, of course, but there's no obstacle to sharing the wealth of the musical scene.

Opera, operetta, concerts, ballet and recitals follow a year-round rhythm. When the opera houses and concert halls

Opera is at its grandest on Margaret Island's open-air stage. Right: Dancers from various regions keep Hungarian folk traditions alive.

close for the summer, outdoor venues take over: grand opera in the Margaret Island open-air theatre, chamber music in the courtyard of a Baroque mansion, broad comic opera in the remains of an ancient monastery within a modern hotel. Though the performances are impeccable by any standards, and the costumes resplendent, tickets remain relatively affordable compared with the prices in many western capitals.

To quicken the pace of cultural life, there are annual festivals and special events. The Budapest Spring Festival in March shows off the best in Hungarian music, dancing and art. In late September and October, Budapest Art Weeks provide the framework for special concerts and theatrical programmes featuring famous foreign artists.

Folklore also goes outdoors in summer, but most nights one or another company of

Hungarian dancers—amateur or professional—can be seen on stage at the Municipal Folklore Centre, Fehérvári út 47 in the southern part of Buda (XI). The dancers, in brilliant costumes, are full of spirit and enthusiasm—just like the music. They can even sing while they whirl and stomp their boots. The accompaniment may be provided by a large orchestra including a cymbalom, an instrument related to the dulcimer with a tone resembling at times a banjo, harp or harpsichord; it's a thrill to hear when a master performs at hair-raising speed. The repertoire runs from the *csárdás* to boot-slapping Lads' Dances, wedding dances and dances devised in the 18th century to lure country bumpkins to army recruiting officers.

The schedules of operas, concerts, folklore performances and other attractions of interest to foreign tourists are published in *Programme in Hungary,* issued free every month with text printed in both German and English. It also lists major jazz and pop concerts, as well as rock concerts approved for young people which take place in summer.

For other popular doings, look for announcements on walls, light posts or pillars.

Hungarians, who all have to study film appreciation in school, are keen film-goers, and in Budapest there are regular screenings of English and American films in their original versions.

Turning to the racier side of Budapest nightlife, establishments with names as exotic as the Moulin Rouge and Maxim's present international floor-shows with big production numbers, including glamorous, minimally dressed dancers. Nowadays almost anything goes. The nightclubs open at 10 p.m. and keep going, noisily and expensively, until 4 or 5 a.m. Elsewhere in town, mostly in and near the major hotels, are nightspots with dancing but no show. You'll also notice scores of discotheques and inviting, dimly-lit bars, which keep late hours.

For visitors who prefer the excitements of the gambling casino, the Budapest Hilton provides roulette, baccarat, blackjack and slot machines, while the Lido offers roulette and slot machines. Transactions are no longer only in deutsche marks, but also in Forint and other foreign currencies. Most of the conversation is in German, except for the obligatory *"Faites vos jeux, messieurs".*

Wining and Dining

Hungarians savour life's pleasures more than most people, perhaps because their long history has seen so many defeats and deprivations. When it comes to eating and drinking, they don't miss a chance to reaffirm the joy of living. The most modest restaurant posts a 50- or 60-item menu every day, and the food is as good as it is abundant. The wines maintain a 2,000-year record of excellence. And the service is quick and attentive. In addition, when the waiter adds up the bill, there's no need for foreboding. By the standards of western Europe, it's all a bargain.

Because paprika has been associated with Hungarian cooking for several hundred years, many foreigners imagine that Magyars wake up to goulash and gulp hot peppers the rest of the day. On the contrary, the use of condiments tends to be subtle, with inspired combinations.

Choosing a Restaurant

Hungary's 18,000 or so eating places are divided into a dozen or more categories, none of them, unfortunately, called a "restaurant". If you see the sign "restaurant", it normally means foreign tourists are catered for. Such establishments may even have a menu in English and French in addition to the usual German and Hungarian.

An *étterem* serves a wide range of food and drinks, the prices pegged to the classification bestowed on it—luxury, first, second or third class. A *vendéglő* also provides food and drinks; the decor is often rustic and prices are moderate. Gypsy musicians usually lurk in both types of restaurant at dinner time.

Among the other types of eating places: a *bisztró* is small and reasonably priced; a *büfé* serves hot and cold snacks; a *csárda* is a country inn, often complete with regional atmosphere and romantic music; an *önkiszolgáló* is a self-service snack-bar; and a *snackbar* is an *önkiszolgáló* with pretensions.

In the 1980s, the government franchised many eating places (with less than a dozen employees) to private operators. The profit motive has upgraded them, while the competition has encouraged the standard state-run establishments to do better.

By law, all eating places must offer at least two set

vided for the benefit of foreign clients.

The *à la carte* menu is long and complicated, in keeping with the Hungarian enthusiasm for fine food. Even if you find a menu translated into a language you understand, a certain amount of confusion is inevitable. The lists are organized with categories where Hungarians expect to find them. Thus, desserts are normally printed on the first, not the last page. Drinks often appear on a separate list and may be served by a different waiter.

When to Eat

Breakfast *(reggeli)* is served between 7 and 10 a.m. Most establishments provide a "continental" version—bread and rolls, butter and jam, coffee or tea. However, some hotels routinely add eggs, cold meats, cheese and yoghurt.

Lunch *(ebéd)* is eaten between noon and 2 or 3 p.m. It's the main meal of the day for most people. This means soup, a main course and dessert, with beer or wine or soft drinks, followed by coffee.

At dinner *(vacsora)*, from 7 to 10 or 11 p.m., people usually skip the soup and may forego the meat course for a cold plate. Wine is the most popu-

Gypsy violins are an inevitable part of a night out in Budapest.

menus *(napi menü)* every day. These low-priced "package deals" usually include soup, a main course and dessert.

96 Translations are rarely pro-

lar accompaniment, and while lunchers often stretch it with mineral water, the dinner wine is drunk undiluted.

Hungarian Cuisine

The first Magyars cooked their food in a pot over an open fire. New seasonings and nuances came from France, Italy and Turkey. Paprika was introduced from America in the 17th century, developing over the years into the characteristic piquant, red condiment. The spice is available in "hot" and mild varieties, and although it's the keystone of Hungarian cuisine, many dishes contain no paprika at all. Most food is cooked in lard or rendered fat rather than oil or butter, which sometimes taxes delicate stomachs unaccustomed to the Hungarian method.

Some specialities worth looking for:

Appetizers *(előételek)*. For starters try *libamáj-pástétom,* a flaky pastry shell filled with goose-liver paté mixed with butter and béchamel sauce, spices and brandy. *Hortobágyi húsos palacsinta* (pancakes Hortobágy style)—thin pancakes filled with minced meat and dressed with sour cream—make a delicious beginning to a meal. A vegetarian speciality, *paprika-szeletek körözöttel*

töltve, combines sliced green peppers, ewe's cheese, spices and a dash of beer.

Soup *(levesek)*. *Gulyásleves* (goulash soup) is the real thing: chunks of beef, potatoes, onion, tomatoes and peppers, with paprika, caraway seeds and garlic for added flavour. (Note that what is called goulash abroad is a Hungarian meat stew actually named *pörkölt.*) *Szegedi halászlé* (Szeged fisherman's soup) is a sort of paprika-crazed freshwater bouillabaisse: pieces of giant pike-perch and carp boiled in a stock lengthily concocted from fish heads, tails and bones, with onions and, of course, paprika. On a hot summer day, sample *hideg almaleves* (cold apple soup): creamy and refreshing with a dash of cinnamon.

Fish *(halételek)*. *Paprikás ponty* (carp in paprika sauce) and *pisztráng tejszín-mártásban* (trout baked in cream) show the extremes to which the Hungarians go to glamorize their lake and river fish. *Balatoni fogas* (pike-perch from Lake Balaton) is considered a prime delicacy. (Note that some of the fish are equipped with an infinity of tiny bones, slowing the eating.)

Meat *(húsételek)*. *Fatányéros* (mixed grill) combines oversized chunks of pork, beef, veal and perhaps goose liver, roasted over a spit and served on a wooden platter. *Csikós tokány*, called a cowboy dish, consists of strips of beef braised in a mixture of diced bacon, onions, sliced pepper and tomatoes, served with *galuska* (miniature dumplings). Finally, what could be more Hungarian than *töltött paprika* (stuffed pepper)? Green peppers are filled with minced pork, rice, onions, garlic and then blanketed in tomato sauce.

Game and fowl *(vadak, szárnyasok)*. The Hungarian treatment enhances tastes as rich as *vaddisznó* (wild boar) and *őz* (venison). As for poultry, you'll surely be offered *csirkepaprikás* (chicken paprika), with the two main ingredients of the title—plus onion, green peppers, tomato and sour cream.

Sweets *(tészták)*. Do strive to save some strength for the last course, for the Hungarians excel at desserts. The microscopically thin pastry of *rétes* or strudel ought to be framed in the bakers' hall of fame. The adjectives (and fillings) to look for: *almás* (apple), *mákos* (poppy-seed), *meggyes* (sour cherry) and *túrós* (cottage cheese). Or you could go the

whole hog with *Gundel palacsinta*, named after a famed restaurant owner: pancakes filled with a nut-and-raisin paste, drenched in a creamy chocolate and rum sauce and then flambéed. For simpler tastes there are ice-cream *(fagylalt)*, cheese *(sajt)* or fruit *(gyümölcs)*.

Hungarian Wines

Most of the wine made in Hungary is white, the most famous and inimitable being Tokay *(Tokaji* on the bottle). The volcanic soil of the Tokay region, in north-east Hungary, has produced a wine fit for kings since the Middle Ages. It was a favourite of Catherine the Great and Louis XIV, and inspired poetry from Voltaire and song from Schubert. Some prosaic specifications: *Tokaji furmint* is dry; *Tokaji szamorodni*, medium-sweet; and the full-bodied *Tokaji aszú*, very sweet. The quality is graded from 3 to 5 *puttonyos* (points).

Less celebrated but perfectly satisfying white wines come from the Lake Balaton region. Look for the prefixes "Badacsonyi", "Balatonfüredi" and "Csopaki". The Roman emperors liked Balaton wines so much they had them shipped to Rome.

The best known Hungarian

red, *Egri bikavér* (Bull's Blood of Eger), is a full-bodied hearty wine. More subtle are the *pinot noir* from the same town of Eger and a splendid *Villányi burgundi*.

Budapest waiters are most helpful about wines, so don't hesitate to ask for a recommendation when you order your meal.

Budapest's stately coffee houses serve memorable strudel snacks.

Other Drinks

Hungarian beers go well with heavy, spicy food. Or you have the choice of brews from Czechoslovakia, Austria, Germany or elsewhere in Europe. Well-known international soft drinks are bottled in Hungary, competing with local fizzy products and fruit juices.

Espresso coffee—strong, black, hot and usually sweet —is consumed day and night. There's no alternative except for tea, made to undemanding

standards with familiar brands of imported tea-bags. (The closest you can get to white coffee in most Budapest bars is a tiny cup of espresso with a mini-pitcher of milk or cream on the side.)

As an aperitif you may be offered a "puszta cocktail", menacingly blending apricot brandy, digestive bitters and Tokay sweet wine. After dinner, you may want to compare some of Hungary's extraordinarily good fruit brandies *pálinka)*. Look for *alma* (apple), *barack* (apricot), *cseresznye* (cherry), *körte* (pear) and *szilva* (plum). And now you know what all those beautiful orchards are for.

Tipping

Tipping is very much a fact of life in Hungary today. If you have been served well, which is most probable in almost any Budapest restaurant, it's customary to tip the waiter 10 to 15 per cent. The waiter who brings the bill and takes your money is probably not the one who served you, but don't worry; all the gratuities are pooled.

To Help You Order...

Could we have a table?	**Lenne szabad asztaluk?**
The bill, please.	**Kérem a számlát.**
Keep the change.	**A többi a magáé.**

I'd like...		**Kérnék...**	
beer	**sört**	noodles	**metéltet**
bread	**kenyeret**	potatoes	**burgonyát**
butter	**vajat**	rice	**rizst**
cheese	**sajtot**	salad	**salátát**
coffee	**kávét**	salt	**sót**
fish	**halat**	sandwich	**szendvicset**
fruit juice	**gyümölcslét**	soup	**levest**
lemonade	**limonádét**	sugar	**cukrot**
meat	**húst**	tea	**teát**
milk	**tejet**	vegetables	**főzeléket**
mineral water	**ásványvizet**	water	**vizet**
mustard	**mustárt**	wine	**bort**

...and Read the Menu

alma	apple	kacsa	duck
aranygaluska	sweet dumpling	káposzta	cabbage
ananász	pineapple	kappan	capon
bableves	bean soup	kapucineres	coffee
bakonyi	"outlaw" soup	felfújt	soufflé
betyárleves		kolbászfélék	sausages
bárányhús	lamb	liba	goose
békacomb	frog's legs	málna	raspberries
borda	chop	marhahús	beef
borjúhús	veal	meggy	sour cherries
burgonya	potatoes	narancs	orange
citrom	lemon	nyelvhal	sole
cseresznye	cherries	nyúl	rabbit
csirke	chicken	őszibarack	peach
csuka	pike	palacsinta	pancakes
dinsztelve	braised	paradicsom	tomatoes
dió	nuts	ponty	carp
disznóhús	pork	pörkölt	stew
édeskömény	caraway seeds	pulyka	turkey
eper	strawberries	ráksaláta	crab salad
erőleves	consommé	ribizli	red currants
húsgombóccal	with meat	rántva	breaded
	dumplings	rostélyos	stewed steak
fasírozott	meatballs	saláta	lettuce
fogas	pike-perch	sárgabarack	apricot
fokhagyma	garlic	sárgarépa	carrots
főve	broiled	sonka	ham
galuska	dumplings	sülve	roasted
gesztenye	chestnuts	sültk-	chips (French
gomba	mushrooms	rumpli	fries)
görögdinnye	watermelon	sütve	fried
gulyásleves	goulash	töltött	stuffed
	(soup)	uborka	cucumber
hagyma	onions	vegyesfőzelék	mixed
halsaláta	fish salad		vegetables
húsleves	meat soup	zeller	celery
italok	drinks	zöldborsó	peas

BLUEPRINT for a Perfect Trip

How to Get There
Although the fares and conditions described below have all been carefully checked, it is advisable to consult a travel agent for the latest information.

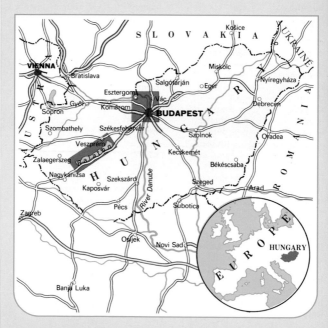

BY AIR

Scheduled Flights

Scheduled service departs daily from London to Budapest. You can fly direct, or via Rome or Frankfurt, but there may be an extra charge for flights routed through Vienna.

Direct flights operate from New York on certain days of the week, and connecting flights are available from major cities in the U.S. and Canada—some of them every day.

Charter Flights and Package Tours

From the United Kingdom: Several British companies organize packages to Budapest. These holidays usually last for seven nights and include bed, breakfast and the cost of a visa, perhaps even a half-day sightseeing tour. Weekend trips are also available.

From North America: Package tours to Warsaw, Vienna and Prague make stops in Budapest. These combined tours last for two weeks and include round-trip air fares and hotels, plus meals and services as specified in each itinerary.

BY RAIL

Trains leave from London's Victoria station every morning, arriving at Budapest the following afternoon. The most direct route is via Dover to Ostend and Vienna. Otherwise you can change stations in Paris and continue on the legendary Orient Express by way of Strasbourg, Stuttgart, Munich, Salzburg and Vienna. Bookings should be made several months in advance for this popular train, and even on the Ostend route you must reserve your seat.

An Interrail card available to travellers under 26 and valid for a month of unlimited travel in most European countries costs little more than the fare to Budapest. The Rail Europ Senior Card (obtainable before departure only) entitles senior citizens to purchase rail tickets for European destinations at a discount.

BY HYDROFOIL

From May through to mid-September a hydrofoil service operates daily on the River Danube from Vienna, with departures three times a week in April and until the end of October. Travel time to Budapest averages 4 ½ hours.

When to Go

Hungary crows about its 2,000 hours of sunshine per year, higher than the average for Central Europe. The best time to catch some of that sunshine is in the summer, when both temperatures and tourism are at a peak. July and August tend to be the warmest and sunniest months, but mild temperatures usually hold from early May to the end of October.

Hotel rates are reduced during the off-season, but no other special advantages await tourists in winter. All the attractions of Budapest continue year-round. Even the theatrical and operatic season keeps going in the summer at open-air locations.

Average monthly temperatures in Budapest:

	J	F	M	A	M	J	J	A	S	O	N	D
°F	27	34	43	54	63	68	72	72	64	52	43	34
°C	-3	1	6	12	17	20	22	22	18	11	6	1

Planning Your Budget

To give you an idea of what to expect, here's a list of some average prices in Hungarian forints—Ft. (except in those cases where prices are normally quoted in U.S. dollars). They can only be regarded as *approximate*, however, as inflation pushes the cost of living ever higher.

Airport transfer. Taxi to central Budapest Ft. 1,200-1,400, airline bus Ft. 100.

Camping. Daily rate per person with car and tent or caravan (trailer) from Ft. 500.

Car hire. $20-100 per day plus $0.25-1.00 per kilometre.

Cigarettes (per packet of 20). Hungarian Ft. 30-40, Western (made in Hungary under licence) Ft. 80-100, Western (imported) Ft. 120-180.

Entertainment. Theatre Ft. 500 and up, opera Ft. 600 and up, discotheque Ft. 100-500, nightclub (minimum) Ft. 300 per person.

Excursions. Half-day Ft. 500, full-day to Ft. 1,000.

Hairdresser. *Woman's* haircut Ft. 500, shampoo and set or blow-dry Ft. 700-800, permanent wave from Ft. 700. *Man's* haircut Ft. 250-300.

Hotels (direct reservation, double room with bath and breakfast). ★★★★★ $150-300, ★★★$60-125, ★$15-25.

Meals and drinks. Lunch in moderate restaurant approx. Ft. 800, in expensive restaurant Ft. 1,500. Dinner *à la carte*, moderate Ft. 1,000, expensive Ft. 2,500. Bottle of wine, expensive Ft. 400, beer Ft. 120, soft drink Ft. 80-100.

Supermarket. Bread Ft. 35 per kilo, litre of milk Ft. 21, butter Ft. 50 for 250 grams, cheese Ft. 300 per kilo, instant coffee (imported) Ft. 100 for 50 grams, salami Ft. 550 per kilo, eggs Ft. 70 per dozen.

Transport. City bus Ft. 15, tram Ft. 12, metro Ft. 12. Sample taxi fares: Castle District to Heroes' Square (Hősök tere) Ft. 250-350, Vigadó tér to Opera Ft. 100-120.

An A-Z Summary of Practical Information and Facts

> A star (*) following an entry indicates that relevant prices are to be found on page 105.
>
> Listed after many entries is the appropriate Hungarian translation, usually in the singular, plus a number of phrases that should help you when seeking assistance.

A   **ACCOMMODATION.** See also CAMPING. It's prudent to book accommodation well in advance, for rooms are often in short supply. The busiest season is the summer, but crowds also descend for trade fairs, exhibitions and major international conferences when you might not expect them. If you arrive without a reservation, though, all is not lost. Staff at tourist information or travel agency offices at the airport, railway stations and border-crossing points can usually help with finding accommodation—in a private home if all else fails.

Hotels* (*szálloda*) are graded by the star system: a five-star hotel is truly luxurious, and a one-star budget hotel has few amenities. Except for the very top international hotels in Budapest, don't expect air conditioning, swimming pools or saunas. Most hotels in the three-to-five star class have their own shopping arcades, tourist agency and airline offices and a variety of sightseeing programmes. Hotel rates can drop by as much as 30% outside the summer tourist season.

Accommodation in **private homes**—a room with or without breakfast, or a self-contained **flat**—can be booked through travel agencies in Budapest and other towns. The rates in Budapest are about the same as those of moderate hotels, but lower in the country.

The equivalent of English "Bed and Breakfast" establishments are found along major roads and in holiday centres. Often the sign *Szoba kiadó* is supplemented by its German equivalent, *Zimmer frei* ("rooms available"). You don't need a travel agency or reservation; just knock on the door.

I'd like a single room/ double room.	**Egyágyas/Kétágyas szobát kérek.**
with bath/with shower	**fürdőszobával/zuhanyozóval**
What's the daily rate?	**Mibe kerül naponta?**

AIRPORT* (*repülőtér*). International flights operate mostly from Budapest's Ferihegy Airport, the country's biggest commercial airfield; there are also smaller airports throughout the country. Among the facilities at Ferihegy: porters, baggage trolleys, currency exchange desks, accommodation and car hire desks, a news-stand, a buffet and restaurant, a post office with international telegraph service and a duty-free shop. Terminal 1 serves foreign airlines, while Terminal 2 is reserved for the use of MALÉV, the Hungarian national airline.

It takes three quarters of an hour to travel from the airport to the centre of Budapest. MALÉV operates an airport bus service between Ferihegy (on the south-east outskirts of Budapest) and the Engels tér bus terminal (platform 1):

Ferihegy-Budapest centre, every half hour from 6 a.m. to 10.30 p.m.
Budapest centre-Ferihegy, every half hour from 5 a.m. to 9 p.m.

Where do I get the bus to the city centre/to the airport?	**Hol a buszmegálló a városközpont felé/a repülőtér felé?**

BABY-SITTERS. Except for the luxury hotels, which can usually arrange for baby-sitters and provide cots, highchairs, etc., this could be a problem, since no organized sitter service exists in Hungary. It may come to mobilizing one of the hotel maids or a friend of the desk clerk, and there may well be a language problem.

Can you get me/us a baby-sitter for tonight?	**Tudna nekem/nekünk biztosítani ma estére egy baby-sittert?**

CAMPING* (*kemping*). Budapest has two large camping grounds, but the country's biggest concentration of sites is around Lake Balaton. All told there are more than 280 campsites in Hungary. They are generally open between May 1 and the end of September. Each site is graded according to international standards. The top (three-star) sites have more facilities, a larger area for each family, and tents and cabins for hire.

A list of the major campsites and their facilities—from supermarkets and currency exchange offices to beaches and night-clubs—along with a detailed map is issued by the Hungarian Camping and Caravanning Club (*Magyar Camping és Caravanning Club—MCCC*): Üllői út 6, H-1088 Budapest VIII.; tel. 1336-536

CAR HIRE*. See also Driving. Hiring a car in Hungary involves no special problems; arrangements and conditions are similar to those encountered elsewhere. The minimum age requirement is 21, and the driver

C should be in possession of a valid licence, held for at least one year. A deposit has to be paid, though this is normally waived for holders of accepted credit cards. Bills must be settled in hard currency. All cars are insured, but supplementary coverage is available at an extra charge. By advance arrangement the car may be dropped off at another Hungarian town or in another country for an extra fee.

As well as state agencies such as Cooptourist, Főtaxi and Volántourist, both Hertz and Europcar operate directly in Hungary. In addition, a number of private Hungarian car hire companies have been set up. Cars, with or without drivers, may be booked either directly through these agencies or through travel bureaux in hotels, at the airport, etc.

I'd like to hire a car.	**Egy kocsit szeretnék bérelni.**
large/small	**nagy/kis**

CIGARETTES, CIGARS, TOBACCO* (*cigaretta, szivar, dohány*). Shops called *Dohánybolt* or *Trafik* stock tobacco products, as do most hotels and supermarkets. A wide range of cigarettes from Hungary and neighbouring countries, as well as well-known international brands, is available at relatively advantageous prices. Intertourist shops sell some hard-to-get foreign brands for hard currency.

Restrictions on smoking cover most public places, including all cinemas, theatres and concert halls. Smoking is banned on public transport, including the ticket and waiting-room areas of railway stations. But long-distance trains have some smoking carriages.

I'd like a packet of cigarettes.	**Kérek egy csomag cigarettát.**
filter-tipped	**filteres**
without filter	**filter nélküli**
A box of matches, please.	**Egy doboz gyufát kérek.**

CLIMATE and CLOTHING. Hungary's vaunted temperate climate is subject to fluctuation. While the average July temperature may look flawless at 20°C (68°F), the mercury can lurch into tropical swelter or down to a very brisk chill with little warning. So summer visitors should pack for all eventualities. Raincoats may also be useful some summer nights. In winter, be prepared for snow and bracing cold.

As for formality, a certain Middle European seriousness persists, though there are no definite rules. Evening gowns and dark suits are standard at the Opera House, but jeans are also acceptable. On warm summer days, jackets and ties are abandoned in most areas of life. Headwaiters don't discriminate against informally dressed clients. For official or business meetings, suits are the norm.

Post offices (*postahivatal*). Local post offices are usually open from 8 a.m. to 5 p.m., Monday to Friday, and until noon or 1 p.m. on Saturdays. Main post offices operate from 7 a.m. until 8 p.m., Monday to Saturday. In Budapest, there are 24-hour offices at the Eastern (Keleti) and Western (Nyugati) train stations.

Post offices handle mail, telephone, telegraph and telex services—the major ones also telefax (facsimile)—but neither international money transfers nor aerogramme service. Stamps (*bélyeg*) can sometimes be bought at tobacconists or where postcards are sold. Postboxes are painted red and are usually decorated with a hunting horn.

Telephone (*telefon*), **telegrams** (*távirat*) **and telex**. Coin telephones for local calls are yellow or grey, while those for international calls are red. Illustrated, self-explanatory instructions are posted. Long-distance and international calls are best made through your hotel switchboard or at a post office.

A modern international telecommunications centre with all telephone, telegraph, telex and telefax services operates at the corner of Petőfi Sándor utca and Martinelli tér (Budapest V) from 7 a.m. to 8 p.m., Monday to Friday, and until 7 p.m. on Saturdays, with limited service on Sunday mornings and public holidays.

Directory enquiries in foreign languages, tel. 1172- 200.

express (special delivery)	**expressz küldemény**
registered	**ajánlott**
airmail	**légiposta**
I'd like a stamp for this letter/	**Kérek egy bélyeget erre a levélre/**
this postcard, please.	**a képeslapra.**
I'd like to send a telegram.	**Táviratot szeretnék feladni.**

COMPLAINTS. Every establishement in Hungary has a "complaint book" (*vásárlók könyve*) on the premises, but problems are resolved slowly through such channels. It's much wiser to try to sort out any difficulties face-to-face with the manager. Above all, relax and keep your temper in check. Threats will get you nowhere, while patient good humour is always a good policy.

CONVERTER CHARTS. Hungary uses the metric system. The only slight variation from standard European practice is that most products in food markets are sold and labelled in dekagrams rather than grams (10 **109**

C dekagrams = 100 grams = 3 ½ ounces). For fluid and distance measures, see pp. 113/114.

Temperature

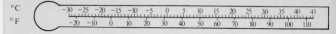

Length

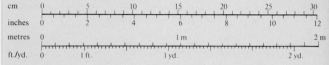

Weight

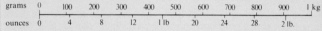

CRIME and THEFT. Though violent crime is rare in Hungary, visitors ought to take elementary precautions to protect their property. This means locking car doors and hotel rooms. When you park your car, place valuables out of sight or lock them in the luggage compartment. Don't leave jewellery, money or documents in your hotel room; use the hotel's safe instead. And be alert in public transport: your pockets and purse may seem attractive to quite proficient thieves.

CUSTOMS (*vám*) **and ENTRY REGULATIONS.** See also DRIVING. Everyone needs a valid passport to visit Hungary. For visa regulations it's best to contact the Hungarian consulate in your own country. Visas can be obtained through travel agents or direct from any Hungarian diplomatic mission—it usually takes less than 24 hours. As long as you aren't travelling by train, you can arrive without a visa and be given one at the frontier or airport. Visas are valid for visits of up to 30 days, and can be extended.

Green and red customs channels are in use at the airport and at the main western border towns such as Hegyeshalom. If you have nothing to declare, use the green lane (spot checks do take place). Here are the main items you may take into Hungary duty-free and, upon your return home, into your own country:

Into:	Cigarettes		Cigars		Tobacco	Spirits		Wine	
Hungary	250	or	50	or	250g.	1	l. and	2	l.
Australia	250	or	250g	or	250g.	1	l. or	1	l.
Canada	200	and	50	and	900g.	1.1	l. or	1.1	l.
Eire	200	or	50	or	250g.	1	l. and	2	l.
N. Zealand	200	or	50	or	250g.	1	l. and	4.5	l.
S. Africa	400	and	50	and	250g.	1	l. and	2	l.
U.K.	200	or	50	or	250g.	1	l. and	2	l.
U.S.A.	200	and	100	and	*	1	l. or	1	l.
* a reasonable quantity.									

Among the items forbidden: narcotics, explosives, weapons.

Currency restrictions. Visitors may be required to report the currencies they're carrying, though there is no limit on the foreign funds permitted. As for Hungarian currency, no more than 500 forints in coins and/or bank-notes may be brought in or taken out. Note that there is a restriction on the amount of forints that may be re-exchanged when leaving the country.

Registration. If you're staying at an hotel, campsite or officially recognized guest accommodation, registration will be done automatically. (You'll have to leave your passport at the hotel desk overnight.) If you stay in private accommodation, you need register only if you wish to remain more than 30 days.

Leaving Hungary. The customs officer may ask what you're taking out of the country in the way of commodities and currencies (see also VAT below). Keep handy all sales slips and currency exchange receipts. Aside from museum-worthy antiques and works of art, which require special permits for export, the only customs problem which might surprise you concerns food: you can take out of Hungary only enough food to be used during your travels, up to a value of 500 forints. Salami hoarders beware! For full details on the ins and outs of customs regulations, see the leaflets available at travel agencies and hotels.

VAT. VAT (sales tax) of 25% is included in the purchase price of most goods in Hungary. Foreign tourists buying a minimum 25,000-forint worth of goods in one shop at one time can ask for a VAT certificate, have it **111**

C stamped at the border customs and claim back the VAT amount in hard currency—providing hard currency was paid.

I have nothing to declare.   **Nincs elvámolni valóm.**

D **DRIVING IN HUNGARY.** To take your car into Hungary you need: passport and visa; valid driving licence; car registration papers; adequate insurance.

Cars from most European countries are automatically considered to be fully insured, with these exceptions: vehicles from France, Italy, Portugal, Spain, Greece, Turkey and Iceland, which must carry proof of insurance ("green card").

Driving regulations. Cars must be fitted with a nationality plate or sticker and rubber mudguards. You are required to carry a set of spare bulbs, a first-aid kit and a red warning triangle for display in case of an accident or breakdown. The driver and front-seat passenger must use seat belts; children under 12 are prohibited from travelling in the front seat. Drivers and passengers of motorcycles and scooters have to wear crash helmets, and use dimmed headlights at all times. It is against the law to lend a foreign-registered car to anyone, be it a Hungarian resident or another tourist.

Drive on the right and pass on the left. Hungary's accident rate is one of Europe's highest. Drive with special vigilance until you've had time to take the measure of the local drivers. At road crossings where signs indicate no priorities, the vehicle on the right has the right of way. Pedestrians have the right of way at pedestrian crossings, marked with white stripes. (If you're a pedestrian, don't count on it!) In built-up areas, blowing the horn is forbidden except, of course, if it helps prevent an accident. At night and when visibility is poor, headlights should be dipped. On any road except a motorway (expressway), be alert for unexpected obstacles—livestock, horse-drawn wagons and bicycles, for instance. These can pose a real danger.

Hungary's expanding motorway system is well maintained and toll free. Yellow emergency telephones, for use in case of breakdown or accident, are spaced every 2 kilometres (1¼ miles) along the Budapest–Balaton expressway.

Speed limits. Limits are 120 kilometres per hour (75 mph) on motorways, 100 kph (60 mph) on highways, 80 kph (50 mph) on country roads, and 60 kph (37 mph) within residential areas. Limits are lower for buses, heavy **112** lorries, cars towing caravans (trailers) and motorcycles.

The police are strict about speeding. You could be fined 1,000 forints on the spot for exceeding the limit, with considerably higher penalties for what's considered dangerous speeding.

Alcohol. In Hungary, drinking and driving are totally, dangerously incompatible. The permissible limit for blood alcohol content is zero; even a glass of beer rings the bell. The law is especially severe on anyone causing an accident while under the influence of alcohol, and on hit-and-run drivers. Foreigners receive no leniency in these cases. Otherwise, the traffic police are very helpful and considerate to foreign tourists.

Fuel and oil (*benzin; olaj*). Filling stations are distributed along the motorways and main roads at intervals of 10 to 30 kilometres. On minor roads, they are up to 50 kilometres apart. Stations are usually open from 6 a.m. to 10 p.m. All-night service is available at all Shell and at some major ÁFOR stations. Fuel generally comes in three octane ratings—98, 92, 86—and unleaded (rare). Brands available are ÁFOR, AGIP, ARAL, BP and Shell. Staff at most service stations will change your oil or wash your car, but they are rarely equipped for handling repairs.

Fluid measures

Parking. The use of parking meters is widespread in central Budapest. Most allow parking at will, but in the area of greatest congestion, bright red 60-minute meters have been installed. However, be careful: in some streets, parking—and even traffic—is not permitted. Elsewhere in urban areas, there are automatic parking-ticket vending machines, or you may be approached by parking attendants who collect a fee and issue official receipts. If you leave your car in a prohibited zone so as to impede traffic, it will quickly be towed away by the police.

Road signs and signposts. Standard international pictographs relate information and warnings on all Hungarian roads. Motorways are indicated by green signs, all other main roads by dark blue.

D **Distances.** Here are some approximate road distances in kilometres between Budapest and some regional centres and border-crossing points of interest to users of this guide:

Balatonfüred	130	Rábafüzes	250
Esztergom	60	Siófok	105
Hegyeshalom	170	Sopron	210
Keszthely	155	Visegrád	45

To convert kilometres to miles:

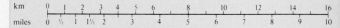

Breakdowns/Accidents. Remember to put out the red warning triangle 50 yards behind your car. Accidents must be reported—to the police in case of personal injury. Cars with damaged bodywork are allowed out of the country only if they have an official certificate for the damage.

The "yellow angels" of the Hungarian Automobile Club (*Magyar Autóklub*) come to the rescue of any driver in distress on any major road. They do on-the-spot repairs—free for members of affiliated auto clubs. But finding spare parts for Western-made cars can be a problem of availability as well as of price. The Automobile Club also offers a wide range of services—information, insurance, reservations, guided tours, legal advice. The Club's headquarters is at:

Budapest II, Rómer Flóris u. 4/a; tel. 1152-040

For 24-hour breakdown service in Budapest, telephone 2528-000

Full tank, please.	**Kérem, töltse tele a tankot.**
Check the oil/the tires/ the battery, please.	**Ellenőrizze az olajat/a gumikat/az akkumulátort.**
I've had a breakdown.	**Meghibásodott a kocsim.**
There's been an accident.	**Baleset történt.**
Can I park here?	**Szabad itt parkolnom?**

E **ELECTRIC CURRENT.** Throughout Hungary the current is 220-volt, 50-cycle A.C. Plugs are the standard continental type, for which British and North American appliances need an adaptor.

EMBASSIES and CONSULATES (*nagykövetség; konzulátus*)

Canada Budapest II, Budakeszi üt 32; tel. 1767-711

| **Great Britain** | Budapest V, Harmincad u. 6; tel. 1182-888 | E |
| **U.S.A.** | Budapest V, Szabadság tér 12; tel. 1126-450 | |

EMERGENCIES. See also EMBASSIES AND CONSULATES, HEALTH AND MEDICAL CARE, POLICE, etc.

Emergency telephone numbers throughout Hungary:

Ambulance	04
Fire	05
Police	07

GUIDES and INTERPRETERS (*idegenvezető; tolmács*). Guides/inter- G
preters can be hired by the day or half-day through travel agencies in
Budapest. These guides, however, may not be qualified to handle the more
difficult linguistic problems that arise in certain business or technical dis-
cussions. State organizations dealing with foreigners usually provide staff
interpreters for such occasions.

| We'd like an English-/French-/ | **Egy angolul/franciául/németül** |
| German-speaking guide. | **beszélő idegenvezetőt kérünk.** |

HAIRDRESSERS and BARBERS* (*fodrász; borbély*). Even in small H
neighbourhood shops the service is expert and accommodating ... and very
cheap by Western standards. "First-class" establishments in the luxury
hotels charge higher prices. Tipping is customary; give about 15%.

haircut	**hajvágás**
shampoo and set	**mosás és berakás**
shampoo and blow-dry	**mosás és szárítás**
permanent wave	**tartós hullám**
colour rinse	**festés**
manicure	**Kézápolás**

Not too short.	**Ne nagyon rövidre.**
A little more off (here).	**(Itt) Egy kicsit többet kérek**
	levágni.

HEALTH and MEDICAL CARE. Many visitors come to Budapest from
abroad to regain their health at the therapeutic baths which make this one
of the leading European spa cities. But if an accident or sudden illness
should interfere with your holiday, the Hungarian National Health Service
(abbreviated *Sz. T. K.*) and the emergency squad (*Mentők*) are well
equipped to handle any unexpected problems. Most Hungarian doctors and
dentists also have private practices. To find one, ask at your hotel desk or **115**

H at your consulate, which will have a list of local doctors who speak your language.

It is perfectly safe to drink tap water (*csapvíz*) in Budapest.

Pharmacies. Look for the sign *gyógyszertár* or *patika*. In Hungary these shops sell only pharmaceutical and related products—not the wide assortment of goods available in their British or American counterparts. (For cosmetics and toiletries, go to an *illatszerbolt*; for photo supplies, to a *fotószaküzlet*.)

Several Budapest pharmacies stay open round the clock. Their addresses are always displayed on an illuminated sign in the window of all other pharmacies.

Where's the nearest pharmacy?	**Hol a legközelebbi patika?**
I need a doctor/dentist.	**Orvosra/Fogorvosra van szükségem.**
I have a pain here.	**Itt fáj.**
headache	**fejfájás**
stomach ache	**gyomorfájás**
a fever	**láz**
a cold	**megfázás**

HITCH-HIKING (*autóstop*). It may be legal, but hitch-hiking is not encouraged—and getting lifts may prove difficult. To compensate, Hungary's public transport is not that expensive.

HOURS. See also COMMUNICATIONS and MONEY MATTERS. Most shops are open from 10 a.m. (some food shops from 6 or 7 a.m.) to 6 p.m., Monday to Friday, and until 2 p.m. on Saturdays. Only a few establishments—mostly tobacconists, florists and pastry shops—stay open on Sundays. Department stores operate from 9 a.m. to 7 p.m., Monday to Friday, and until 2 p.m. on Saturdays. Department stores and many shops are open until 8 p.m. on Thursdays. In Budapest, there are numerous 24-hour food shops.

Hairdressers work from as early as 6 or 7 a.m. to as late as 9 p.m., Monday to Friday, until 4 p.m. on Saturdays.

Museums generally are open from 10 a.m. to 6 p.m., daily except Mondays and certain holidays (admission free on Saturdays). Some small museums operate fewer hours, so it's best to check before you go.

L **LANGUAGE.** Hungarian, which is totally unrelated to the languages of surrounding countries, is the mother tongue of more than 95% of the population. The people speak very clearly, without slurs or swallowed sounds;

since every word is stressed on the first syllable, a sort of monotone often ensues.

By far the most widely known foreign language is German. A minority of Hungarians (mostly the younger generation) know English, and even fewer know some French. Until 1989—when it ceased to be a compulsory subject—Russian was taught to all Hungarians for 4–8 years in school.

The Berlitz phrase book HUNGARIAN FOR TRAVELLERS covers most of the situations you are likely to encounter in Hungary. To get you started, here are the most commonly noted signs you'll see:

bejárat	entrance
eladó	for sale
húzni	pull
kijárat	exit
műemlék	monument
nyitva	open
tilos	prohibited
tolni	push
zárva	closed

And a phrase or two:

Do you speak English/French/ German?	**Beszél Ön angolul/franciául/ németül?**
Good morning	**Jó reggelt**
Good afternoon	**Jó napot**
Good evening	**Jó estét**
Good night	**Jó éjszakát**
Thank you	**Köszönöm**

LAUNDRY and DRY-CLEANING (*mosoda; vegytisztító*). Hotels usually take care of laundry and cleaning problems with dispatch. If you're staying elsewhere, look for the sign *Patyolat*, which indicates an establishment handling both laundry and dry-cleaning. The larger shops may offer express service.

When will it be ready?	**Mikor lesz kész?**
I must have this for tomorrow morning.	**Erre holnap reggelre van szükségem**.

LOST PROPERTY. A central bureau, Talált Tárgyak Központi Hivatala, deals with lost-and-found problems:

Budapest V Erzsébet tér 5; tel. 1174-961

L A separate office handles property found on vehicles of the Budapest public-transport system:

Budapest VII, Akácfa utca 18; tel. 1226-613

I've lost my wallet/my handbag/ my passport.	**Elvesztettem az irattárcámat/ a kézitáskámat/az útlevelemet.**

M **MAPS.** Travel agencies—and some hotels—give out free maps of Hungary and Budapest. Maps with much more detail, including bus and tram routes, the locations of all theatres, restaurants and public buildings, are sold at news-stands, bookstores and Budapest public transport offices. The maps in this book were prepared by Cartographia of Budapest.

I'd like a street map.	**Egy várostérképet kérnék.**
I'd like a road map of this region.	**Egy erre a vidékre vonatkozó térképet kérnék.**

MEETING PEOPLE. Hungarians are open and friendly. They are so helpful to foreigners that, if you unfold a map on the street, they may give you directions whether you're lost or not. Because their language is so outlandish, they are genuinely delighted when a foreigner attempts to say a few words in Hungarian.

As for formalities, there is a lot of hand-shaking and kissing on the cheek, and men are still seen to kiss the hand of a lady.

MONEY MATTERS

Currency. The Hungarian *forint* (*Ft.*) is divided into 100 *fillér* (*f*).

Coins: 10, 20 and 50 f and Ft. 1, 2, 5, 10 and 20.
Banknotes: Ft. 10, 20, 50, 100, 500, 1,000 and 5,000.

For details of restrictions on import of Hungarian currency, see CUSTOMS AND ENTRY REGULATIONS.

Banks and currency exchange. Official foreign-exchange facilities are found in most banks, hotels and motels, at larger campsites, at travel agencies and in some department stores. The currency-exchange office of the Central European International Bank is situated in Aranykézutca, in the passage, facing the bank proper.

Banking hours are generally from 9 a.m. to 5 p.m., Monday to Friday, **118** and 9 a.m. to 2 p.m. on Saturdays.

Remember to take your passport with you, and be sure to keep all receipts. To reconvert forints into foreign currency when you leave Hungary, you must show the relevant receipt. For VAT regulations, see p. 111.

It is unwise to sell foreign currency to private citizens; don't be tempted by generous offers in the street—you risk being cheated.

Credit cards and traveller's cheques. Many tourist-oriented establishments—hotels, restaurants, shops, travel agencies—are geared to accept international credit cards; you'll see the signs on the door. Traveller's cheques and Eurocheques are also easy to cash. Some shops, such as Intertourist branches, deal *only* in foreign currency transactions, accepting cash, traveller's cheques and credit cards.

I want to change some pounds/dollars.	**Fontot/Dollárt szeretnék beváltani.**
Do you accept traveller's cheques?	**Traveller's csekket elfogadnak?**
Can I pay with this credit card?	**Ezzel a hitelkártyával fizethetek?**

NEWSPAPERS and MAGAZINES (*újság; folyóirat*). The Hungarian news agency MTI publishes a weekly bilingual English-German paper, *Daily News/Neueste Nachrichten*. It is available from most hotels and on almost every news-stand in Budapest.

Major hotels and news-stands carry Western newspapers and magazines, including the *Times* of London, the *International Herald Tribune* (edited in Paris), and the weeklies *Time* and *Newsweek*. Newspapers from the West usually arrive on the day of publication.

A free monthly magazine, *Programme in Hungary*, has parallel texts in English and German.

The *Hungarian Observer* is an independent monthly magazine covering politics, culture and business in English. The journal *New Hungarian Quarterly*, also in English, offers profound insights into Hungarian life, culture and politics.

Have you any English-language newspapers?	**Van angolnyelvű újságjuk?**

PHOTOGRAPHY. Hungarian shops sell international brands of film, but to be sure you don't run out of your preferred brand, it's wise to carry an adequate supply from home. In Budapest and some provincial cities, quick processing facilities can develop and print your films within an hour or two.

P   The Hungarians are easy about being photographed, but use common sense concerning what, who, when and where. They've stopped advertising military and other sensitive installations with big "no photography" signs, but they're still taboo for camera fans. Some airport security machines use X-rays which can ruin your film. Ask that it be checked separately, or enclose it in a lead-lined bag.

I'd like some film for this camera.	**Ehhez a géphez kérnék filmet.**
Black-and-white film	**fekete fehér film**
colour prints	**színes kópiák**
colour slides	**színes diák**
35-mm	**harmincöt milliméter**

How long will it take to develop this film?	**Meddig tart előhívni ezt a filmet?**
May I take a picture?	**Lefényképezhetem?**

POLICE (*rendőrség*). See also EMERGENCIES. Police wear blue and grey uniforms. Traffic police and highway patrols dress in a similar manner but with white caps and white leather accessories to make them more visible. Police cars are blue and white. There is no special police unit detailed to deal with tourist enquiries but the police in general are helpful to foreigners.

Where is the nearest police station?	**Hol a legközelebbi rendőrség?**

PUBLIC HOLIDAYS (*hivatalos ünnep*)

January 1	*Újév*	New Year's Day
March 15	*Nemzeti ünnep*	National Holiday
May 1	*A munka ünnepe*	Labour Day
August 20	*Szt. István ünnepe*	St. Stephen's Day
October 23	*Nemzeti ünnep*	National Holiday
December 25	*Karácsony első napja*	Christmas Day
December 26	*Karácsony második napja*	Boxing Day
Movable date:	*Húsvét hétfő*	Easter Monday

Are you open tomorrow?   **Holnap nyitva tartanak?**

R   **RADIO and TV.** Very brief news bulletins for foreigners are broadcast, in summer only, on Budapest Radio and on TV. Leading hotels provide

videos and satellite television.

Hungarian television broadcasts in colour on two channels, daily. On
Channel 2 some imported programmes are transmitted in the original language. Both radio and television carry bundles of commercials from time to time.

To catch up with the news, you'll need a transistor radio powerful enough to pick up European stations on medium wave at night, or the short-wave transmissions of Voice of America, the BBC, Radio Canada International, etc.

RELIGIOUS SERVICES (*istentisztelet*). The great majority of Hungarians are Roman Catholics. Mass is usually said in Hungarian but in Latin, English and German as well. Other religions are also represented, most notably Protestant, Eastern Orthodox and Jewish. Most churches are open to the public. If you visit an historic church for sightseeing purposes while a service is in progress, stay in the rear of the building so as not to disturb the worshippers.

TIME DIFFERENCES. Hungary follows Central European Time, GMT
+ 1. In summer, the clock is put one hour ahead (GMT + 2).

Summer chart:

New York	London	**Budapest**	Jo'burg	Sydney	Auckland
6 a.m.	11 a.m.	**noon**	noon	8 p.m.	10 p.m.

TIPPING. Have no fear of giving offence if you offer a tip: the old custom survives in Hungary, and gratuities are expected by a wide assortment of service personnel, as well as taxi drivers and gypsy violinists. There are no iron-clad formulae for the appropriate amount to give, but waiters and taxi drivers normally get 10%, barbers and women's hairdressers 15%. Here are some further suggestions to save the embarrassment of under- or over-tipping:

Porter, per bag	Ft. 50
Bellboy, errand	Ft 50
Maid, per week	Ft. 300
Doorman, hails cab	Ft. 30
Hat-check	Ft. 30
Lavatory attendant	Ft. 20
Gypsy violinist, for personal attention	Ft. 200-300

T	Tourist guide (half-day)	Ft. 300
	Theatre usher	add Ft. 20 to programme for sale
	Filling station attendant	round up amount on pump (+ Ft. 50 for checking air and oil, Ft. 20-30 for cleaning windscreen)
	Keep the change.	**A többi a magáé.**

TOILETS. Budapest is well supplied with public conveniences—in metro stations, parks and squares, museums and, of course, in hotels, restaurants and cafés. The sign may point to *mosdó* or *W.C.* (pronounced *vay*-tsay), and if pictures don't indicate which room is which, you'll have to remember that *férfi* means "men" and *női* means "women".

| Where are the toilets? | **Hol a W.C.?** |

TOURIST INFORMATION OFFICES (*turista információs iroda*). The Hungarian travel company IBUSZ has offices in some 15 foreign cities, providing information, tour bookings, etc. Among them:

Great Britain   Danube Travel Agency Ltd., General Agent IBUSZ-Hungary,
6 Conduit Street, London W1R 9TG;
tel. (071) 493-0263

U.S.A.   IBUSZ Hungarian Travel Ltd.,One Parker Plaza, Suite 1104, Fort Lee (New York), N.J. 07024; tel. (201) 592-8585

In Budapest and in all tourist areas, IBUSZ and competing travel agencies such as Budapest Tourist, Cooptourist, Siótour and Volántourist, as well as all regional travel agencies, run networks of offices handling money exchange, housing problems, excursions and general information. About 100 such agencies operate in and near hotels, railway stations, busy shopping areas and at the airport. Many are open during normal office hours, but in summer the more important ones stay open until 8 or even 10 p.m.

Tourinform. The Hungarian Tourinform service, situated at Sütő utca 2 in central Budapest, provides information on accommodation, entertainment and other tourist information in English, French, German, Russian and Spanish. You can also call 1179-800 in Budapest to obtain answers to your questions. If you prefer to write, contact Tourinform, P.O.B. 185, **122** -1364 Budapest.

The Tourinform service operates from 7 a.m. to 9 p.m., Monday to Friday, to 8 p.m. on Saturdays and from 8 a.m. to 1 p.m. on Sundays.

Where's there a tourist office?   **Hol találok turista irodát?**

TRANSPORT*. The Budapest Transport Company (*Budapesti Közlekedési Vállalat—BKV*) operates a comprehensive public transport service which commuters of almost any city might envy: fast, clean and stunningly cheap. No place in Budapest is more than 500 metres from a bus, tram, trolley bus or metro stop. Maps of all the lines, both surface and underground, are sold at major stations. A one-day pass is valid for travel on all forms of public transport.

Buses (*busz*). Blue Ikarus buses, made in Hungary, cover some 450 miles on more than 200 routes in Budapest. A bus stop is marked by a blue-bordered rectangular sign with the silhouette of a bus and the letter "M"—for *megálló*. At most stops a sketch map of the route, a list of the stops, the hours of operation and even the minimum and maximum number of minutes between buses are posted. You must have a blue ticket *before* you board a bus. Automatic dispensers sell them at major bus stops and pedestrian subways, or you can buy them at metro change booths, travel bureaux and tobacco shops. Inside the bus, validate your ticket in one of the red punching devices near the doors; keep the serial number facing up. Then hold onto your ticket in case an inspector should ask for it. Though you'll see very few passengers punching tickets, it doesn't mean they're dishonest; the majority buy cheap monthly passes allowing unlimited travel. Signal at the door when you want to get off.

Mini-buses. Mini-buses link modern Budapest with the west bank and serve the Castle District, where they connect with the Cog railway.

Trolley buses (*trolibusz*). To save fuel, these lines are being expanded, but they still constitute only a tiny proportion of the whole municipal system. Use a yellow tram ticket.

Trams (*villamos*). Yellow trams or streetcars, usually in trains of three or four, cover a 120-mile network. Ten of the 50 tram lines run all night. You need a yellow tram ticket which you must validate on board. The same tickets also serve on the suburban railway within the city limits, and the original Millenary underground (subway) line, now called metro No. 1.

Underground (*földalatti* or *metró*). Underground (subway) line No. 1, the Millenary line, was opened in 1896—the first in continental Europe. It operates modern tram-like cars and requires a yellow tram ticket. The new

T metro lines, 2 and 3, use Soviet wide-gauge trains. All three lines converge at Deák tér, but there is no free transfer.

Trains (*vonat*). There are three suburban commuter lines (*HÉV*), of which the Batthyány tér to Szentendre route is of interest to tourists.

Inter-city trains run by Hungarian State Railways (*Magyar Államvasutak—MÁV*) operate from three Budapest stations—the historic Keleti (East) and Nyugati (West) stations and the spacious modern Déli (South) terminal. First- and second-class tickets are sold as well as rail passes good for seven or ten days of unlimited travel within Hungary. (Train compartments are marked 1 and 2.)

Taxis. Metered vehicles both state-owned and private serve Budapest, mostly from taxi ranks near the big hotels, metro and train stations. They can also be hailed on the street when the roof sign saying "Taxi" is lit. Taxis can also be summoned by phone: 1222-222 or 1666-666. Private taxis are usually cleaner and the drivers, more polite.

If you're going beyond the city limits you'll be charged the return fare to the boundary line. Tips are customary.

Boats. Motor launches ply the Budapest section of the Danube from about 9 a.m. to 8 p.m. daily during the tourist season. Among the principal stations are Gellért tér, Batthyány tér and Petofi tér, and there are several stops on Margaret Island. Sightseeing excursion boats operate from Vigadó tér, from where boats and hydrofoils leave for Szentendre, Visegrád and Esztergom.

I want a ticket to ...	**Kérek egy jegyet ... -ba/-be/-ra/-re*.**
single (one-way)	**egy útra**
return (round-trip)	**oda-vissza**
first/second class	**első/másod osztály**
Will you tell me when to get off?	**Megmondaná, mikor szálljak le?**

---

*In Hungarian, prepositions are replaced by suffixes. Choose one that

sounds harmonious with the place name.

SOME USEFUL EXPRESSIONS

yes/no	**igen/nem**
please/thank you	**kérem/köszönöm**
excuse me	**bocsásson meg**
where/when/how	**hol/mikor/hogy**
yesterday/today/tomorrow	**tegnap/ma/holnap**
day/week/month/year	**nap/hét/hónap/év**
left/right	**bal/jobb**
big/small	**nagy/kicsi**
cheap/expensive	**olcsó/drága**
hot/cold	**meleg/hideg**
open/closed	**nyitva/zárva**
free (vacant)/occupied	**szabad/foglalt**

Does anyone here speak English/French/German?	**Van itt valaki aki angolul/franciául/németül beszél?**
I don't understand.	**Nem értem.**
Please write it down.	**Kérem, írja ezt le.**
Waiter!/Waitress!	**Pincér!/Pincérnő!**
I'd like ...	**Kérnék ...**
Just a minute.	**Egy pillanat.**
Help me, please.	**Segítsen kérem.**

NUMBERS

0	**nulla**	13	**tizenhárom**	40	**negyven**
1	**egy**	14	**tizennégy**	50	**ötven**
2	**kettő**	15	**tizenöt**	60	**hatvan**
3	**három**	16	**tizenhat**	70	**hetven**
4	**négy**	17	**tizenhét**	80	**nyolcvan**
5	**öt**	18	**tizennyolc**	90	**kilencven**
6	**hat**	19	**tizenkilenc**	100	**egyszáz**
7	**hét**	20	**húsz**	101	**százegy**
8	**nyolc**	21	**huszonegy**	200	**kettőszáz**
9	**kilenc**	22	**huszonkettő**	300	**háromszáz**
10	**tíz**	23	**huszonhárom**	500	**ötszáz**
11	**tizenegy**	30	**harminc**	1,000	**egyezer**
12	**tizenkettő**	31	**harmincegy**	2,000	**kétezer**

Index

An asterisk (*) next to a page number indicates a map reference.

Andrássy út (Népköztársaság
   útja)   52, 53*, 68, 69
Aquincum   15, 41*, 45, 47

Baths   12-13, 50
   Czászár fürdő   45, 52-53*
   Király fürdő   44, 52-53*
   Rácz fürdő   40
   Rudas fürdő   40, 52-53*
   Széchényi gyógyfürdő   52-53*,
   74
Batthyány tér   43-44
Bridges   10
   Árpád   50, 50*
   Chain (Széchényi Lánchid)   10,
   25*, 43, 52-53*, 60
   Elizabeth (Erzsébet híd)   40,
   52-53*
   Liberty (Szabadság híd)   40,
   52-53*
   Margaret (Margit híd)   44, 48,
   50*, 52-53*

Casinos   94
Castle District   25*, 26-36
Castle of Vajdahunyad (Vajda-
   hunyad vára)   52-53*, 73
Children's Railway (Széchenyi-
   hegyi Gyermekvasút)   37, 41*
Churches
   Basilica (St. Stephen's Parish
   Church, Szent István
   templom)   52-53*, 60
   Franciscan (Ferencesek
   temploma)   52-53*, 57
   Franciscan ruins (Ferences
   templom romjai)   50, 50*

Inner City Parish (Belvárosi
   templom)   51, 52-53*
Matthias (Mátyás-templom)
   25*, 27-28
Premonstratensian Chapel
   (Premontrei templom) 50, 50*
St. Anne's (Szent Anna
   templom)   44, 52-53*
University (Egyetemi templom)
   52-53*, 57
Citadel (Citadella)   36-37,
   52-53*
City Hall (Fővárosi Főpolgarmestri
   Hivatal)   52-53*, 57
City Park (Városliget)   52-53*,
   72-74, 91
Cog railway (fogaskerekű vasút)
   37, 41*
Covered Market   65

Danube Bend (Dunakanyar)
   74-80, 75*
Dominican Convent Ruins
   (Domonkos kolostor romjai)
   48, 50*

Eagle Hill Nature Reserve
   (Sas-hegyi Természetvédelmi
   Terület)   37-38, 41*
Erzsébet tér   52-53*, 59
Esztergom   75*, 78-80

Fishermen's Bastion (Halász-
   bástya)   25*, 29
Folklore   93-94
Fortuna utca   25*, 31

Freedom Square (Szabadság tér)
    52-53*, 62

Great Boulevard (Nagykörút)
    52-53*, 66
Gül Baba türbéje (tomb)
    45, 52-53*

Hercules Villa   41*, 46
Heroes' Square (Hősök tere)
                52-53*, 69-70
Hills   36-38
    Gellért-hegy   15, 36, 41*
    Hármashatár-hegy   37, 41*
    János-hegy   37, 41*
    Liberty (Sváb-hegy)   37, 41*
Hotels   62
    Budapest Hilton   25*, 29, 94
    Gellért   40
    Grand   50, 50*
    Thermal   50, 50*
Houses of Parliament
    (Országház)   52-53*, 63

Kádár, János   24
Kigyó utca   52-53*, 57
Kings
    Béla IV   17-18, 27, 48-49
    Corvinus, Matthias   18
    Louis II   19
    Stephen I   17, 29, 65

Lake Balaton   13, 80-84, 81*
Liszt, Franz   23, 28, 56, 65, 79
Little Boulevard (Kiskörút)   51,
    52-53*, 65

Magyars   17, 23, 97
Margaret, Princess and Saint   50
Margaret Island (Margit-sziget)
    41*, 48-50, 50*, 90, 92
Martinelli tér   52-53*, 56-57

Military Amphitheatre (Katonai
    Amfiteátrum)   41*, 45
Museums, Galleries, Collections
    Applied Arts (Iparművészeti
        Múzeum)   52-53*, 66
    Art Gallery (Műcsarnok)
        52-53*, 72
    Budapest History (Budapesti
        Történeti Múzeum)   25*,
        34-36
    Chinese Art (Kína Múzeum) 52-
        53*, 69
    Commerce and Catering
        (Magyar Kereskedelmi és
        Vendéglátóipari)   25, 31
    East Asian Art (Hopp Ferenc
        Kelet-ázsiai Múzeum)
        52-53*, 69
    Ethnographic (Néprajzi
        Múzeum)   52-53*, 64
    Fine Arts (Szépművészeti
        Múzeum)   11, 52-53*,
        70-71
    Golden Eagle Pharmaceutical
        (Arany Sas Patikamúzeum)
        25*, 32
    Recent History (Magyar
        Munkásmozgalmi Múzeum)
        25*, 36
    Hungarian Agricultural (Magyar
        Mezőgazdasági Múzeum) 73
    Hungarian National (Magyar
        Nemzeti Múzeum)   15,
        52-53*, 65
    Hungarian National Gallery
        (Magyar Nemzeti Galéria)
        25*, 36
    Iron Foundry (Öntödei Múzeum)
        44, 52-53*
    Jewish Religious and Historical
        Collection (Zsidó Múzeum)
        52-53*, 66

Military History (Hadtörténeti Múzeum) *25*, 33*

National Lutheran (Evangélikus Országos Múzeum) *52-53*, 59*

Philatelic (Bélyegmúzeum) *67*

Postal (Postamúzeum) *68*

Roman Camp (Római-tábor Múzeum) *41*, 46*

Semmelweis History of Medicine (Semmelweis Orvostörténeti Múzeum) *40, 42, 52-53**

Transport (Közlekedési Múzeum) *52-53*, 74*

Underground Railway (Földalatti Vasúti Múzeum) *52-53*, 59*

Nagy, Imre *24*

National Sports Swimming Complex (Hajós Alfréd Sportuszoda) *48, 50**

Népstadion (People's Stadium) *12, 88, 90*

New York Café *68*

Obuda *41*, 45-47*

Open-air Theatre (Szabadtéri Színpad) *48, 50**

Országház utca *25*, 32*

Palatinus Outdoor Public Swimming Complex (Palatinus Strand) *48, 50**

Paris Arcade (Párisi udvar) *57*

Railway Stations
Eastern (Keleti pályaudvar) *52-53*, 66*

Southern (Déli pályaudvar) *33*

Western (Nyugati pályaudvar) *52-53*, 68*

Restaurants *95-96*

River Danube (Duna) *8, 25*, 41* 47, 52-53*, 54, 74, 75*, 78-79, 90*

Romans *15-16, 50, 54, 76*

Royal Palace (Budavári palota) *25*, 34-36*

Ski lift (libegő) *37, 41**

Shopping *85-88*

Sports *88-90*

State Opera House (Állami Operaház) *52-53*, 68-69*

Synagogue, former (Régi Zsinagóga) *25*, 31*

Szentendre *74-75, 75**

Táncsics Mihály utca *25*, 31*

Tárnok utca *25*, 31-32*

Tóth Árpád sétány *25*, 32-33*

Úri utca *25*, 32*

Váci utca *52-53*, 54-56*

Vidám Park (Amusement Park) *74*

Vienna Gate (Bécsi kapu) *25*, 31*

Vigadó (concert hall) *56*

Visegrád *75*, 76-78*

Wine *84, 88, 98-99*

Youth Stadium (Ifjúságistadion) *48, 50**

Zoo (Fővárosi Allatkert) *52-53*, 73-74*

INDEX

128